1950—1959

Yearbooks in Science

1950—1959

MONA KERBY

Twenty-First Century Books
A Division of Henry Holt and Company
New York

Twenty-First Century Books
A Division of Henry Holt and Company, Inc.
115 West 18th Street
New York, NY 10011

Henry Holt® and colophon are trademarks of Henry Holt and Company, Inc.
Publishers since 1866

Published in Canada by Fitzhenry & Whiteside Ltd.
195 Allstate Parkway, Markham, Ontario L3R 4T8

Library of Congress Cataloging-in-Publication Data
Yearbooks in science.
p. cm.
Includes indexes.
Contents: 1900–1919 / Tom McGowen — 1920–1929 / David E. Newton — 1930–1939 / Nathan Aaseng — 1940–1949 / Nathan Aaseng — 1950–1959 / Mona Kerby — 1960–1969 / Tom McGowen — 1970–1979 / Geraldine Marshall Gutfreund — 1980–1989 / Robert E. Dunbar — 1990 and beyond / Herma Silverstein.
ISBN 0–8050–3431–5 (v. 1)
1. Science—History—20th century—Juvenile literature. 2. Technology—History—20th century—Juvenile literature. 3. Inventions—History—20th century—Juvenile literature. 4. Scientists—20th century—Juvenile literature. 5. Engineers—20th century—Juvenile literature. [1. Science—History—20th century. 2. Technology—History—20th century.]
Q126.4.Y43 1995 95–17485
609'.04—dc20 CIP
AC

ISBN 0–8050–3435–8
First Edition 1995
Printed in Mexico
All first editions are printed on acid-free paper ∞.
10 9 8 7 6 5 4 3 2 1

Cover design by James Sinclair
Interior design by Kelly Soong

Cover photo credits
Background: Mount Palomar Observatory, Photo Researchers, Inc. **Inset images** (clockwise from right): Polio virus, © OMIKRON/Photo Researchers, Inc.; *Sputnik 2* spacecraft, NOVOSTI/Science Photo Library/ Photo Researchers, Inc.; Fireball from Bikini Atoll test, U.S. Navy/SPL/Photo Researchers, Inc.; Fallout shelter symbol created by James Sinclair; *Zinjanthropus* skull, John Reader/SPL/Photo Researchers, Inc.; Bubble chamber tracks, © OMIKRON/Science Source/Photo Researchers, Inc.

Photo credits
p. 11: Jack Fields/Photo Researchers, Inc.; p. 15: Photo Researchers, Inc.; p. 19 (top): USNO/TSADO/Tom Stack & Associates; p. 19 (inset): NASA; p. 21: David Parker/Science Photo Library/Photo Researchers, Inc.; p. 27, 29, 38, 66, 68, 70: UPI/Bettmann; p. 28: NOVOSTI/SPL/Photo Researchers, Inc.; p. 30, 74: The Bettmann Archive; p. 35: A. Barrington Brown/Photo Researchers, Inc.; p. 42: © Jon Brenneis/Photo Researchers, Inc.; p. 48, 50: March of Dimes Birth Defects Foundation; p. 49: © OMIKRON/Photo Researchers, Inc.; p. 52: © Will & Deni McIntyre/Photo Researchers, Inc.; p. 56 (top): © OMIKRON/Science Source/Photo Researchers, Inc.; p. 56 (bottom): Brookhaven National Laboratory/SPL/Photo Researchers, Inc.

To Jonathan and Kristen Kerby, and
to April, Kyle, and Jonathan Gann

Acknowledgments

Thanks to Western Maryland College physics professor David Guerra for his review of the physics chapter; to Capitol College President G. William Troxler for his review of the technology chapter; and to my mother, Bette Rudd Nolen, whose first intellectual love was science.

Contents

1 Anthropology and Archaeology 9

2 Astronomy, Airplanes, and Spaceflight 17

3 Biology 33

4 Chemistry 41

5 Medicine 45

6 Physics 53

7 Technology 63

Further Reading 75

Index 77

1

Anthropology and Archaeology

Both anthropologists and archaeologists are curious about people. Simply stated, anthropologists study humans while archaeologists study the objects that humans have left behind.

In the 1950s, these scientists were explorers, adventurers, and treasure hunters. Their work took them to faraway places such as the city of Jericho, the continent of Africa, the Mediterranean Sea, the Egyptian pyramids, and to the high plains of Texas.

One question that anthropologists and archaeologists frequently ask is "How old is this?" In the past, this was one riddle that had not been easy to solve. But in the early 1950s, a chemist named Willard Libby was just putting the finishing touches on an instrument that would become one of the most important tools ever used by archaeologists and anthropologists. The instrument gave scientists a way to determine the age of something by measuring the presence of carbon-14. This method was called radiocarbon dating.

Radiocarbon Dating

Take a step back in time and walk into Willard Libby's laboratory of the 1950s. You feel as if you have just stepped into some madman's lab. You see glass containers with bubbling liquids. Pipes are running everywhere. The whole contraption is hissing and steaming. Against the wall, you see huge steel boxes the size of pianos.

Artifacts rest on a table. You see a piece of wood from an Egyptian pharaoh's boat. You see a sandal that was found in an Oregon cave. You are tempted to touch an arrowhead piercing a blackened bone.

Dr. Libby picks up the piece of wood from the pharaoh's boat. He is ready to determine how old it is. What is Dr. Libby's first step in radiocarbon dating? He sets fire to the wood and watches it burn.

Libby was an American chemist. During World War II, he worked on the atomic bomb, and after the war, he began experimenting with radioactivity.

Some fifty years earlier, Nobel Prize winner Ernest Rutherford had discovered a way to measure radioactive decay and to determine the age of rocks. Libby extended this knowledge by figuring out how to determine the age of ancient plants, animals, and humans.

Libby knew that all living things absorb carbon-14. As cosmic rays bombard the earth's atmosphere, they collide with nitrogen atoms, creating tiny quantities of carbon-14. This carbon-14 reaches the earth in the form of carbon dioxide. Plants absorb the carbon dioxide, and the plants are eaten by animals and by humans. Humans also eat the animals. As a result, every living thing has some carbon-14 in it.

Carbon-14, known as radiocarbon, is radioactive. This means that it can be traced. Libby knew that when something dies, the radiocarbon in it decreases at a definite rate. Libby figured out how to determine the age of an object by tracing its radioactive decay.

To determine the age of an archaeological object, Libby would burn a small piece, converting it to carbon dioxide gas. Carbon-14 atoms in the carbon dioxide gas released particles. These particles were then measured by radiation counters. Libby used this measurement to determine the amount of carbon-14 in the original object. (The radiation counters were inside the huge steel boxes the size of pianos.)

Carbon-14 lasts for a certain number of years, and then decay reduces it by half. This time period is called the half-life. The half-life of carbon-14 is about 5,700 years. After another 5,700 years, decay reduces carbon-14 by an additional one-fourth, then an additional one-eighth, and so on.

Radiocarbon dating can't tell you how long something lived. Radiocarbon dating tells you how many years have passed since it did live. As you can see, it's a complicated procedure, yet amazingly enough, radiocarbon dating can date objects that are some 50,000 years old.

During the 1950s, when Libby wanted to test his procedure, he asked archaeologists to give him small pieces of artifacts so that he could burn

Willard Libby, a chemist, developed radiocarbon dating, a crucial procedure used by both archaeologists and anthropologists.

them up and deduce their ages. Believe it or not, the archaeologists were so eager to discover the ages of their treasures that they did just as Libby requested.

There are other ways of determining the ages of things, but Willard Libby's radiocarbon dating is one of the most accurate. In 1960, Dr. Libby received the Nobel Prize in chemistry for his success in the field of archaeology.

The Search for the First Americans

In 1925, a black cowboy named George McJunkin rode out on the range near Folsom, New Mexico. When he spied some bones sticking up from the ground, he got off his horse and started to dig. While he was digging, he also found a spearhead. McJunkin had never seen such bones or such a spearhead in his life.

That day on the range, McJunkin had stumbled over one of the most significant archaeological finds in North America. The bones had belonged to an extinct bison. The spearhead, later named a Folsom point, was prehistoric. This find seemed to prove that humans had been on the North American continent since the Ice Age. In 1951, using the recently invented radiocarbon dating, archaeologists determined that the bison bones were 10,000 years old.

Archaeologists now had a mission. They searched for the remains of early hunters. They were looking for the first Americans.

Soon the search widened. In Mexico, archaeologists found a skull with worn teeth, which they named the Tepexpan man, and estimated its age at 10,000 years. In Texas, archaeologists found a skull that was 12,000 years old. Even though it was a woman's skull the scientists named it the Midland man. In an Oregon cave, archaeologists found some sandals that were 9,000 years old. Who left those sandals, and why?

A theory is an explanation based on observation and reasoning. Perhaps, the scientists reasoned, the first Americans had walked across the Bering Strait from the Asian continent during the last Ice Age. Though the archaeologists of the 1950s searched for prehistoric human remains which would support their theory, they found only hunting sites.

Even today, the search for the oldest Americans continues.

The Puzzle of Linear B

In the 1890s, the archaeologist Sir Arthur Evans explored the ruins of Crete, a Greek island in the Mediterranean Sea. He found several hundred tablets with strange writing that he called Linear B.

The tablets were flat lumps of dull clay. Some were no more than an inch high, and others were tablets about 10 by 5 inches (25 by 13 centimeters). Some of the writing on the tablets was in pictures, or hieroglyphics, while the rest of the writing looked like scribbles.

For forty years, Evans puzzled over Linear B, but he never broke the code. In 1936, Evans gave a speech and mentioned this puzzle. A young boy named Michael Ventris heard that speech.

Ventris grew up. During World War II, he served as a plane navigator, and after the war, he worked as an architect. But he never stopped thinking about Linear B. In his spare time, he worked at solving the puzzle. In 1953, convinced that he had the answer, Ventris published his findings.

Ventris explained that Linear B was an ancient form of Greek that had

A VERY OLD COMPUTER

During a rough storm, a Greek merchant ship sank near Antikythera in the Mediterranean Sea. For the next 2,000 years, it lay buried in its watery grave. In 1900, sponge fishermen discovered the wreckage. Archaeologists studied the ship's holdings; one artifact puzzled them. Some parts were missing, but the artifact looked like a bronze machine with writing inscribed in the metal. Perhaps it had been a navigational tool, the archaeologists suggested.

In 1951, Professor Derek de Solla Price of Yale University decided to take a look. Using X rays, Price and his assistants peered inside the bronze structure, where they saw an assortment of gears. Price realized that they were looking at a 2,000-year-old computer, a computer that showed the ancient sailors the ever-changing positions of the sun, moon, and planets.

In 1987, physicist Allan Bromley and clockmaker Frank Percival made a working replica of the Antikythera Mechanism. Price's theory was correct.

been used around 1400 B.C. This meant that Linear B was nearly 3,000 years old.

What did the writing say? Did it describe great adventures or secret treasures? Not at all. Michael Ventris unlocked the code of Linear B by deciphering lists—lists of livestock, lists of workers, and lists of military equipment.

A Lasting Portrait

In 1952, archaeologist Kathleen Kenyon was up to her knees in mud. Nearby was a giant mud mound that stood 70 feet (21 meters) high. Kenyon was searching for the ancient city of Jericho, in the Middle East, and she didn't stop digging until she hit rock. According to biblical accounts, the first Jericho had been built upon rock.

Kenyon had wanted to find the walls of Jericho, and she did. But she also discovered something else. The original city of Jericho was 8,000 years old. This bears repeating: for 8,000 years, people have lived in the city of Jericho.

Kenyon discovered that these early people knew how to build mud brick homes. They shined their floors and used floor mats. Yet for some reason, they didn't use pottery, as many other early people did.

In 1953, Kenyon uncovered seven human skulls buried underneath a house. Their facial features had been painstakingly molded with clay. One was beautiful. Kenyon theorized that these were sculptures of loved ones, and that this was a way of keeping "portraits" of ancestors, permanently.

Piltdown Man

In the early 1900s, part of a human skull, an apelike lower jaw, and some stone tools were found near Piltdown, England. This event caused great excitement in the scientific world. Scientists called their discovery the Piltdown man and believed that he was the missing link between humans and apes. They estimated the Piltdown man's age at 250,000 years.

But in 1955, after radiocarbon testing, scientists discovered that they had been tricked. The skull probably came from a nearby cemetery and was at best 700 years old. The teeth had been artificially stained, and the jaw belonged to an orangutan. The Piltdown man was a hoax.

Sailing Through Time

More than 4,500 years ago, the great Egyptian king Khufu (Cheops) decided to build three pyramids at Giza, in Egypt. He didn't do the building. He forced thousands of his people to do the work. And Khufu made certain that his personal pyramid was the biggest of the three. When the ancient Greeks saw it, they claimed that it was one of the Seven Wonders of the World. Khufu's pyramid was 482 feet (145 meters) tall—178 feet (54 meters) taller than the Statue of Liberty. Its base covered 13 acres (5 hectares). Inside the pyramid, there were secret passageways and hidden rooms. One of those rooms and its contents stayed secret for 4,500 years.

In 1954, during a cleaning, workers found one of the hidden rooms. The Greek archaeologist Kamal el Mallakh peered into a tiny hole but didn't see anything. "Like a cat," he said, "I closed my eyes. . . . I smelt time. I smelt centuries. I smelt history."

What he smelled was a boat. It seemed King Khufu had decided to bring along not one but two boats for his use in the afterlife.

The boats had been dismantled and stored in two separate chambers. The archaeologists of the 1950s decided to rebuild one of the boats. There were more than 1,200 pieces. The ancient king's carpenters had thoughtfully marked the boards with symbols to show how the parts fit together. Still, it took the modern-day crew sixteen years to rebuild the boat.

By 1970, they had a 142-foot- (43-meter-) long cedar boat with a cabin near the stern. The ends of the boat tilted upward. Some archaeologists

Mary and Louis Leakey, with the Zinjanthropus *skull found at Olduvai Gorge*

believe King Khufu wanted the boats so that he could sail away to his after-life. Other archaeologists believe that these boats were used during the ceremonies at the king's funeral.

The Nutcracker Man

On July 17, 1959, archaeologist Mary Leakey squatted in the dirt and began to dig. She was at her regular place—the Olduvai Gorge in what is now Tanzania, Africa. That morning, she found a piece of a skull and two teeth. She rushed back to camp to show her husband, Louis. Over the course of several months, they found hundreds of skull fragments, which Mary pieced together.

While the Leakeys lovingly called the skull Dear Boy, they gave him the scientific name *Zinjanthropus boisei*, which meant "East African man." Later, when they realized the skull was related to other early human bones found in the area, Dear Boy's scientific name was changed to *Australopithecus boisei*. But none of these names stuck. On account of his large cheeks, the skull became known by his nickname—Nutcracker Man.

The Nutcracker Man wasn't actually a human; he was more like a cousin to early humans. This species was the first to shape stone tools. Eventually, the species would be named *Homo habilis* (handy human). How long ago did the Nutcracker Man live? He lived 1,750,000 years ago—give or take a few years!

2

Astronomy, Airplanes, and Spaceflight

The decade of the fifties included one of the most significant days in the twentieth century. On October 4, 1957, the Russians launched *Sputnik 1*, the world's first artificial satellite. This single event marked the beginning of the space age.

While this was not the only major achievement in space during this decade, *Sputnik*, more than anything else, captured the imagination and fears of the American people.

In this chapter, we'll examine the achievements that preceded *Sputnik*. We'll look at *Sputnik* itself, and finally, we'll see how this twentieth-century phenomenon set the stage for the future of space exploration.

Astronomy

What do you wonder about when you look up at the stars at night? Do you name them? Do you ask what stars are made of or how far away they are? Do you ever think about what lies hidden in the darkness between the stars? Do you wonder how the universe began?

In the 1950s, astronomers wondered about all these ideas. While the questions were simple enough for a child to ask, the answers were not so easy to come by.

In this decade, there were two major theories on how the universe began. One was called the big bang theory, and the other was called the steady state theory. Scientists argued about which theory was right.

Yet many astronomers didn't even take sides in the debate. Instead, they concentrated on their discoveries. For them, cosmology—the study of the universe in space and time through exploration of the past, present, and future—had too many theories and too few facts.

But in science, theories are as necessary as facts. And in the 1950s, both were equally fascinating.

Discoveries in Astronomy

The decade opened with the announcement that Pluto was the second smallest planet in the solar system, with a diameter of 3,500 miles (5,600 kilometers). (This is about the distance between Seattle, Washington, and Miami, Florida.) A year later, in 1951, Jupiter's twelfth moon, named Ananke, was discovered. In that same year, astronomers had the first proof of something they had long suspected. The dark space between the stars was filled with hydrogen gas.

Hydrogen comes from Greek words meaning "water-former." It is the lightest and simplest chemical element as well as one of the most important. Hydrogen atoms emit radiation, which can be detected by a radio telescope.

The discovery of hydrogen gas in outer space was important for several reasons. One, a theory was on its way to becoming a fact; and scientists always enjoy facts. Two, the discovery offered further proof in favor of using radio telescopes in astronomy; they could "see" billions of light-years farther than optical telescopes.

And three, the discovery of hydrogen gas in space led to new theories. In 1953, astronomers claimed that the universe was twice as big and twice as old as they had previously believed. By 1955, astronomers estimated the universe to be nearly six billion years old, and in 1959, they said it was some ten billion years old.

Both estimates were wrong. Astronomers didn't discover their mistake, however, for another thirty-five years. In 1994, a new generation of astronomers studying photographs taken in space by the Hubble Space Telescope realized that the universe was neither as big nor as old as they had believed.

But let's get back to the 1950s. Besides trying to figure out the age of the universe, astronomers were also trying to figure out what it looked like. Before then, astronomers didn't even know the shape of our own Milky Way

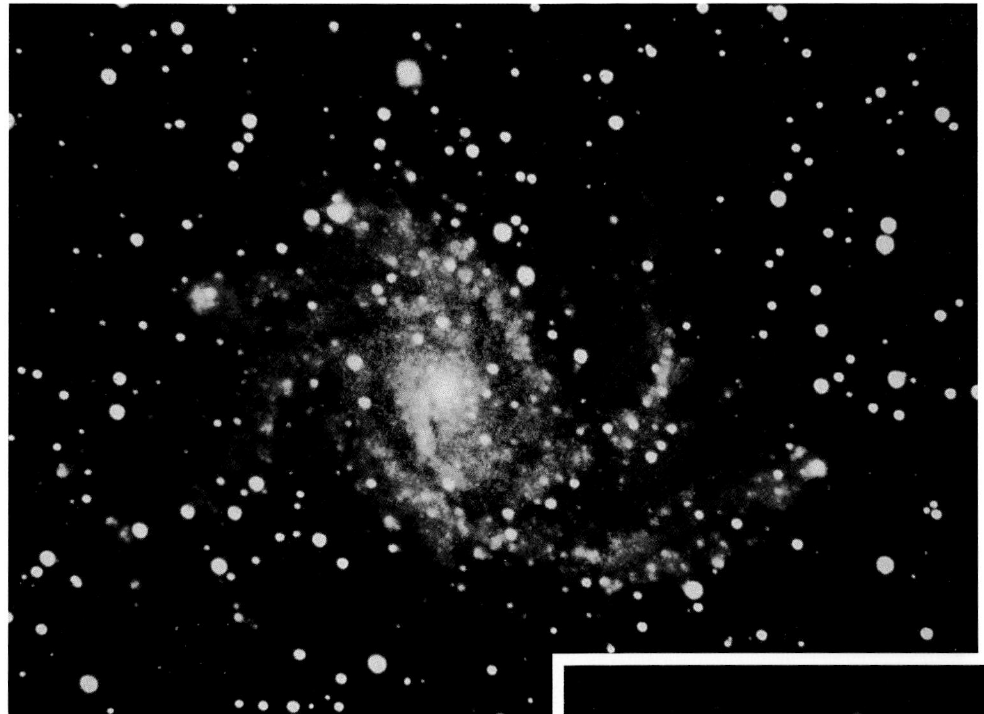

In the early 1950s, scientists believed that the Milky Way was a spiral galaxy, shaped very much like this one.

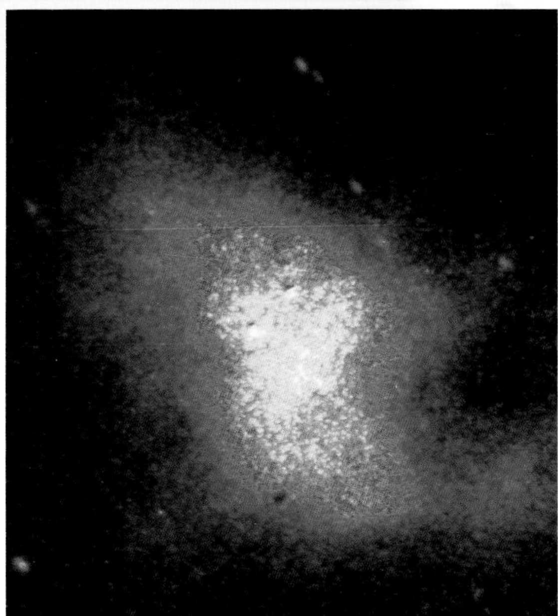

The Crab Nebula, shown here in an ultraviolet image, is the rapidly expanding remains of an exploding star.

galaxy. In 1951, by measuring radio waves, ultraviolet light, visible light, and X rays coming from the galaxy, astronomers had enough evidence to suggest that the Milky Way was a spiral galaxy.

A spiral galaxy resembles a pinwheel, with a bulge in the center and spiral arms extending outward from the bulge. Astronomers realized that our sun was located in one of the Milky Way's spiral arms.

In 1955, astronomers believed they witnessed the birth of stars when two new ones appeared in the Orion Nebula. This event was significant because it implied that stars are being formed all the time.

But one puzzle of the 1950s did not get solved. Why was radiation coming from the Crab Nebula? In A.D. 1054, scientists in China had recorded the explosion of a star. The Crab Nebula appeared to be the remains of that star. Astronomers in 1956 wondered why this gaseous cloud emitted such strong radiation. They worked to come up with an answer but did not succeed. There would be no more clues to this puzzle until pulsars were discovered in 1967.

Astronomers in the fifties made some important discoveries. These discoveries occurred primarily because of remarkable improvements in telescopes.

The Radio Telescope

The radio telescope was not a new idea. In 1931, when Karl Jansky heard unexplained hissing in transatlantic radio messages, he realized that objects in space emit radio waves. A few years later, Grote Reber built the first radio telescope. But when World War II broke out, scientists helped the war effort by developing ways to track enemy planes. During those years, radio astronomy took a backseat to radar.

After the war, however, scientists once again focused on the heavens. One of these astronomers was Bernard Lovell. In 1951, in Manchester, England, Lovell and some others began building the largest radio telescope in the world.

What exactly is a radio telescope? Lovell's telescope was a gigantic 250-foot (75-meter) "dish" with a big antenna stuck in the middle. To pick up radio waves from space, the device needed to be turned in the proper direc-

RADIO INTERFEROMETERS

While radio telescopes can "see" much farther than optical telescopes, their pictures are sometimes blurry. In 1953, Roger C. Jennison came up with an idea. To bring an object into sharper focus, Jennison developed a way to connect two radio telescopes and to focus them on the same object. This was called a radio interferometer. But because Jennison was "just" a graduate student, his idea was ignored and was not rediscovered until 1975, by Alan E. L. Rogers.

Bernard Lovell, in a photograph taken in 1987. Visible through the window behind him is part of the world's first giant dish radio telescope, which took six years to build.

tion. No one could figure out how to move it, until one of the astronomers came up with the idea of putting the whole thing on an old turret rack from a battleship. It worked.

Stars and other objects in space emit radio waves. But this doesn't mean that outer space creatures are sending us messages. Both light waves and radio waves are forms of radiation. Radio telescopes "see" by tracking the radio waves of objects in space. Radio telescopes can't send signals; they can only receive them.

Lovell's radio telescope picked up radio waves, which were translated into pictures. The pictures were blurry. Even today, the optical telescope gets a clearer image than the radio telescope.

But what makes the radio telescope so wonderful is that it can see billions of light-years past what the optical telescope can see. The reason it can see so far is because it's collecting radio waves, not beams of light.

When you use an optical telescope, the thing you are looking at has to be giving off light. When it's cloudy, it's tough to use an optical telescope. A radio telescope works just fine in cloudy weather.

It took Lovell and his crew six years to build their radio telescope. Meanwhile, halfway across the world, nestled among the pine trees on Mount Palomar in California, work was being done with another telescope. It was an optical telescope, one of the finest in the world. And the astronomers using that telescope were making some startling discoveries.

The Optical Telescope

The white dome rose fourteen stories high on Mount Palomar and housed an optical telescope. Inside the dome, a huge steel horseshoe held a 17-foot (5-meter) concave mirror. The glass mirror weighed 15 tons (14 metric tons). Its size allowed astronomers to focus on faint objects of light, which were then photographed.

The astronomers worked at night, alone, recording what they saw in the sky. Every evening, one astronomer walked up a narrow flight of stairs past the mirror. The astronomer walked along a ramp, and then crawled into a cherry picker—a sort of a crane with a bucket that moved to a tiny observational cage. Here, without much room to stretch, the astronomer stood and studied the heavens.

In 1954, one of those astronomers was a young man named Allan Sandage. That summer, *Fortune* magazine ran a story about scientists. The article included a picture of Sandage and said, "He is helping to define the age and structure of the universe."

Think about it. This is a powerful statement. What was this young man doing up on Mount Palomar?

Sandage was continuing the work that Edwin Hubble began in the 1920s and 1930s. Hubble believed that the universe was expanding. In the fifties, Allan Sandage sat up on Mount Palomar and measured the distances between stars. He was measuring redshifts, which occur when an object of

SANDAGE SPEAKS OUT

In a grandiose style, *Fortune* magazine wrote that the young Sandage was unlocking the secrets of the universe. What did Allan Sandage have to say after a lifetime of work? "Science is full of false clues. There are more false clues than correct ones."

light is moving away from the observer. His somewhat boring task led to one of the biggest debates of the 1950s.

This brings us back to the two theories we mentioned at the beginning of this chapter. It brings us back to a simple yet profound question. How did the universe begin?

The Big Bang Theory

According to the big bang theory, the universe began billions of years ago in a gigantic explosion. The explosion was infinitely hot and dense. Since then, the universe has been expanding, thinning out, and cooling.

Advocates of the big bang theory divided themselves into three groups. Some astronomers believed in an "open universe," where the universe expands forever. The second group of astronomers believed in a "closed universe," where the universe reaches its greatest size and then starts collapsing. The third group believed in a "flat universe," which is somewhere between a closed and an open universe.

The big bang theory was based in part on Hubble's demonstration that the stars were moving away from the big bang explosion. But this theory ignored another simple yet profound question. What was before the explosion?

HOW THE BIG BANG THEORY GOT ITS NAME

Years ago, on a popular British radio show, Fred Hoyle was explaining his steady state theory. When he mentioned the other theory—of how the universe began with an explosion—he called it the "big bang theory." The name stuck. The big bang theorists never cared for Hoyle's term.

The Steady State Theory

In the steady state theory, the universe does not change in time. The universe was the same in the past as it is now and as it will be in the future. The steady state model was based on Aristotle's concept of the universe.

During the 1950s, one of the most vocal defenders of the steady state theory was Fred Hoyle. In spite of Hoyle's efforts, however, evidence favored the big bang evolutionary model.

Fred Hoyle, Bernard Lovell, and Allan Sandage were just a few of the astronomers of the fifties. They were courageous men, and they expressed that courage in their ideas.

At the same time, there was another group of courageous men at work. They weren't particularly interested in ideas. Instead, they took to the skies and confronted fear; they "pushed the edge of the envelope." These men expressed their courage in action. Who were they?

They were test pilots, of course.

Airplanes

One word best describes the airplanes of the fifties—fast. Never before had humans flown so fast or so high.

This new speed was the result of improvements in the plane. From nose to tail, the plane was virtually redesigned. It was rebuilt with stronger metals. The plane's body and wings became graceful and sleek, which reduced air friction and increased speed. Jet engines replaced propeller-driven engines, and this resulted in still more speed and more climbing power. Other improvements included speed brakes, cabin pressurization, and ejection seats.

But all these improvements required one key ingredient—the test pilot. Until the pilot flew the plane, no one knew for sure whether a new design was an improvement or a disaster.

Pushing the Edge of the Envelope

In southeastern California, the Mojave Desert stretches for miles. It is a huge, lonely wasteland. Edwards Air Force Base, located in the western part of the desert, covers some 301,000 acres (120,000 hectares). It's a good place to make secret test flights.

And that's exactly what was happening in the early 1950s. In those days, many pilots "pushed the edge of the envelope." This meant they flew as fast as they could and hoped the plane didn't explode.

The work was dangerous, and yet the young men seemed to revel in it. Sometimes the plane exploded in midair. Sometimes it crashed on landing. Sometimes the plane flew just fine. In 1952, during a thirty-six-week training course, sixty-two pilots were killed.

The "old man" in the crowd of test pilots was Chuck Yeager. He was barely thirty when he set a new world record. On December 12, 1953, Yeager took off in the Bell X-1A. That day, he pushed the edge of the envelope and lived to tell about it. Yeager flew two and one-half times the speed of sound.

A New Vocabulary for Fast Planes

So how fast is two and one-half times the speed of sound? While the answer depends on the altitude of the flying object, Yeager clocked in at faster than 1,600 miles (2,575 kilometers) per hour.

In the fifties, people needed new ways of describing this speed, and they started using words such as *Mach 1*, *supersonic*, *transonic*, and *subsonic*.

Before Austrian physicist Ernst Mach died in 1916, he studied how objects moved at high speeds through gases. Mach developed a way of measuring those speeds in terms of the speed of sound.

The speed of sound is not always the same. At higher altitudes and in cooler temperatures, sound travels at a slower rate. At sea level, the speed of sound is about 740 miles (1,192 kilometers) per hour. At 40,000 feet (12,000 meters), sound travels approximately 660 miles (1,063 kilometers) per hour.

But in 1916, humans weren't traveling that fast or that high, and no one paid much attention to Mach's work. Until the fifties, that is. Then, scientists started using Mach numbers to describe the speed of planes. To get the number, the plane's speed is divided by the speed of sound at the plane's altitude. Mach 1 speed is the speed of sound, or transonic. Speeds greater than Mach 1 are supersonic speeds, which means the plane is flying faster than the speed of sound. Speeds less than Mach 1 are subsonic speeds, or slower than the speed of sound.

Once planes began flying at supersonic speeds, two more vocabulary terms were needed: *sonic boom* and *shock waves*. When a supersonic airplane flew overhead, people on the ground *heard* it. (Remember, Mach numbers measure sound.) There was a terrific bang, or sonic boom. Sometimes people heard two sonic booms a couple of seconds apart. The first was from the airplane's front, and the second was from the plane's rear.

The pilot felt the shock waves. When the test pilot hit Mach 1 speed, he felt a tremendous shudder—a strong pressure disturbance—in the nose of the plane and then another one at the rear of the plane.

The first few times this happened, the planes exploded. Engineers redesigned the planes, streamlining them and building them with stronger metals. As we've already mentioned, each new design had to be tested by a pilot.

OTHER ACHIEVEMENTS IN AIRPLANES

The U.S. Air Force pilots weren't the only ones who were setting records. In 1952, the U.S. Navy announced that it had been conducting its own secret test flights. A year earlier, a navy pilot had reached a speed of 1,300 miles (2,093 kilometers) per hour. That same year, Great Britain started the first jet airline service, carrying passengers between Great Britain and South Africa.

In 1953, the "Pogo" fighter plane made headlines. This plane took off straight up and landed tail first.

Disaster struck again in 1956. The Bell X-2 exploded after it reportedly reached a speed of 2,100 miles (3,380 kilometers) per hour and an altitude of 126,000 feet, or 23 miles (37,800 meters, or 37 kilometers).

On July 16, 1957, U.S. Marine Major John Glenn set a new transcontinental speed record when he flew from California to New York in 3 hours, 23 minutes, and 8.4 seconds.

The test pilots of the fifties were extraordinarily brave. But even though the pilots went high and fast, they never left the earth's atmosphere.

Meanwhile, rocket scientists were setting their own records. During the 1950s, the Pershing rockets flew 450 miles (725 kilometers) into the air. The Jupiter rockets reached the whopping height of 1,600 miles (2,580 kilometers). Sometimes the rockets carried mice or monkeys, but no humans. No one knew if humans could survive in outer space.

It's a good possibility that we might never have known the answer. But on October 4, 1957, the Russians launched *Sputnik 1*. And this event changed the future of the world.

Sputnik launched the space age, an exciting period of exploration and discovery that would lead to a man on the moon. But in 1957, *Sputnik* shocked the nation. People were afraid.

Why? Well, there were several reasons. One, it was the first artificial satellite in the history of humankind that had ever orbited the earth. Two, America was in the midst of a cold war with the Soviet Union, and both sides were stockpiling missiles. Throughout the 1950s, the United States government had continued to build bombs and to explode them. With *Sputnik 1* in orbit, however, Americans jumped to the conclusion that the Soviet Union now had the technological know-how to kill millions of Americans, and the Russians didn't even have to leave home to do it.

A reporter with the *New York Times* wrote that the United States was in a "race for survival." Future president Lyndon B. Johnson, who was then Senate majority leader, claimed that whoever controlled the "high ground of space" controlled the world. In short, the nation panicked.

Sputnik 1 certainly didn't look very scary. It was just 23 inches (58 cen-

Sputnik 1 *is shown here, mounted on a stand, in one of the first official photos of the satellite, taken just before it was launched.*

timeters) in diameter, about the size of a beach ball. It had four skinny antennas that pointed to earth. One set of antennas measured 8 feet (2.4 meters) long, and the other set measured 9 feet (2.7 meters). Inside the satellite, a radio transmitter kept up a steady beep-beeping sound. The whole contraption weighed 184 pounds (83 kilograms).

Sputnik is the Russian word for "traveler," and that's exactly what it did. The tiny traveler had a speed of 18,000 miles (29,000 kilometers) per hour. Every ninety-six minutes, it made another orbit of the earth. From Chicago to the Antarctic Ocean, radio operators started picking up the beep-beeping signals. In Great Britain, Bernard Lovell tracked *Sputnik* with his newly finished radio telescope.

Sputnik should not have caught the Americans by surprise. The period from July 1957 to December 1958 had been named the International Geophysical Year (IGY) by the world's leading scientists. In a spirit of goodwill, the scientists agreed to share their knowledge about earth and its surroundings. In the summer of 1957, that's exactly what the Russian scientists did. No one seemed particularly interested, until suddenly, there was *Sputnik*, orbiting earth and making its merry little beeps. Only now the beeps sounded threatening.

For the first time that anybody could remember, the whole country got interested in science. Congress went to work. President Eisenhower signed bills, and before long, there was money for a space program, and there was money for science programs in schools. *Sputnik* had ushered in the space age.

While Americans agreed that this was a "race for survival," there was dis-

LAIKA, THE FIRST DOG IN SPACE

A month after *Sputnik*, the Russians launched *Sputnik II* with a passenger. Laika, the first dog in space, was a black-and-white mongrel fox terrier. She was decked out in her own space suit and had room to stand, lie down, or sit. She had a dispenser for food. A rubber attachment on her rear caught her bodily wastes. A small electric fan kept her cool.

Laika had enough food for a week, and then she died. If a dog could survive in space, then maybe, scientists reasoned, humans could too.

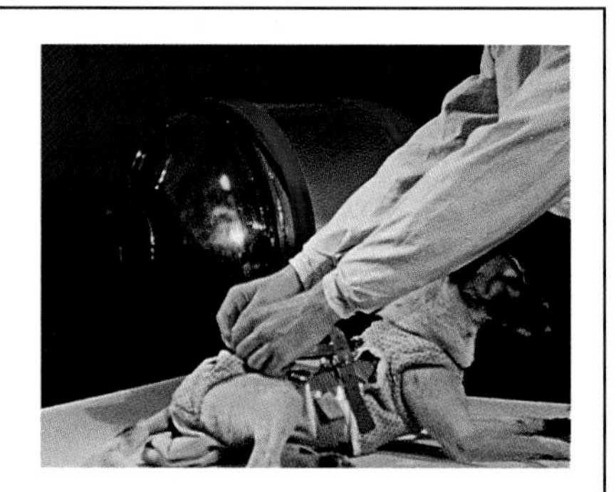

A technician prepares Laika for her launch aboard Sputnik 2 *on November 3, 1957.*

agreement between scientists and politicians about which space program to back. In the end, they decided to use the military's Vanguard rockets. This was a mistake.

On Friday, December 6, 1957, the world watched as the United States launched its first satellite. It rose 6 inches (15 centimeters) off the launchpad and exploded.

The newspapers had a field day. Headlines all over the world poked fun at America's disaster. Some read KAPUTNIK! or STAYPUTNIK! Others claimed that the Vanguard was a rearguard.

After that fiasco, President Eisenhower said that Wernher von Braun (the former German rocket scientist) and his team at Huntsville, Alabama, could have a try. On January 31, 1958, von Braun used a Redstone rocket and launched *Explorer 1*.

Scientists celebrating the successful launch of Explorer 1 *are Wernher von Braun* (right), *James Van Allen* (middle), *and William Pickering, director of the Jet Propulsion Laboratory at the California Institute of Technology.*

> **AN IDEA BEFORE ITS TIME**
>
> Before the military's Vanguard rockets were chosen as the focus of America's space program, some scientist wanted the Dyna-Soar, a space airplane that was boosted into orbit by a rocket and then landed like a plane. The idea was not a dinosaur; it was simply ahead of its time. The Dyna-Soar became a model for the space shuttle of the 1970s.

Explorer 1 was bullet-shaped and weighed 30.8 pounds (13.9 kilograms). The scientific instruments weighed only 11 pounds (5 kilograms). The Russians laughed. They called it the "little grapefruit."

But that little grapefruit worked. In fact, *Explorer 1* kept on working for six years. (*Sputnik 1* had fallen from orbit after four months.)

The instruments on board *Explorer 1* were reliable, sophisticated, and

America's first astronauts were introduced at a press conference in April 1959. John H. Glenn Jr. (third from right) *would become the first American to orbit the earth in 1962.*

tiny. One instrument was installed at the request of James Van Allen. It was a Geiger counter, designed to measure the amount of radiation in the atmosphere. This was an important experiment.

Was there really radiation in space? Scientists discovered that belts of radiation (later known as the Van Allen radiation belts) surrounded the equator and trapped particles from the earth's magnetic fields. Was this radiation dangerous to humans? Could humans survive in space? These questions would not be answered until the next decade.

While *Explorer 1* was a success, *Sputnik* was what Americans remembered and feared. The space race was on, and Americans were not about to be left behind in the dust.

In 1958, the United States established the National Aeronautics and Space Administration (NASA). NASA was independent of the military and warfare; its goal was science. Rocket development, said President Eisenhower, should be used to advance humankind.

On April 9, 1959, the officials at NASA called a press conference. Seven men walked on stage. For a moment, before the room exploded with questions from the reporters, no one spoke. The seven men were Alan B. Shepard Jr., Virgil I. Grissom, L. Gordon Cooper, Walter M. Schirra Jr., Donald K. Slayton, John H. Glenn Jr., and Scott Carpenter. Who were these men?

They were astronauts.

In that moment, the scientists and the test pilots of the 1950s united in a common goal. They were off to search the heavens. And to beat the Russians, of course.

3

BIOLOGY

Let's do a quick review of biology. Biology is the scientific study of living things. The two main divisions of biology are zoology, which is the study of animals, and botany, which is the study of plants. Both zoology and botany lead to further divisions of biology.

In a manner of speaking, biology in the 1950s was like a big box of chocolates. There was something for everyone. For the first time, people were getting a peek at the underwater world, thanks to oceanographer and filmmaker Jacques Cousteau and his crew on the research ship the *Calypso*.

In 1951, biologists discovered that baby chicks grew faster when they were given a dose of antibiotics and vitamin B_{12}. This was good news for chicken farmers. When children ate those chickens, their bodies also developed faster but, unfortunately, it was years before anyone made this connection.

In 1955, biologists studying camels in the Sahara found out that camel humps don't hold water. The reason that camels can survive in the desert heat without drinking is because they don't sweat. In 1957, other biologists discovered that garlic juice stops the growth of cancer in rats. In 1958, still other biologists discovered that cockroaches are carriers of human diseases.

And in 1959, Ilya Darevsky found female lizards in southern Armenia that give birth even though their eggs are not fertilized by male lizards. This process is called parthenogenesis, which in Greek means "virgin birth."

But if you think quick-growing chicks, cool camels, garlic-drinking rats, and virgin lizards are the high points of the 1950s, keep on reading. These stories and others took a backseat to the most significant biological achievement of the entire twentieth century. It was the discovery of DNA.

Something important was happening inside cells—something so powerful that it affected every living thing. In the 1950s, biologists and chemists believed that they had figured out the secret of life.

MAJOR FIELDS IN BIOLOGY

- ***Bacteriology***, the study of bacteria
- ***Biochemistry***, the study of the chemical substances in living things
- ***Biophysics***, the application of the tools of physics to the study of living things
- ***Cryobiology***, the study of how extreme cold affects living things
- ***Cytology***, the study of what goes on inside the cell
- ***Ecology***, the study of the relationships of living things with one another and with the environment
- ***Entomology***, the study of insects
- ***Herpetology***, the study of reptiles and amphibians
- ***Ichthyology***, the study of fish
- ***Microbiology***, the examination of microscopic organisms
- ***Molecular Biology***, the analysis of what goes on inside cells
- ***Ornithology***, the study of birds

The secret was found in the molecular structure of deoxyribonucleic acid, or DNA. DNA is a genetic code. It makes a dog a dog, a cat a cat, a human a human. In fact, it makes you different from every other person on earth.

After the discovery of DNA's structure, many scientists in the 1950s believed that all the important questions in molecular biology had been answered. One scientist disagreed, but she was ignored.

In this chapter, we'll tell the story of DNA. We'll examine what scientist Barbara McClintock had to say. And then, we'll turn to the work of another scientist. She was a biologist and an ecologist, and her name was Rachel Carson.

The Story of DNA

On a spring morning in 1953, at Cambridge University in Great Britain, two biochemists silently eyed a large metal model. To ordinary people, the structure looked like a barbed wire fence that had fought with a hurricane and lost. But James D. Watson and Francis Crick were not ordinary.

For two years, the young American Watson and the Englishman Crick had been trying to figure out the structure of DNA. At last, on that spring morning in 1953, Watson put the final touches to the wire model. When Crick examined it, Watson wrote later, "My stomach felt uneasy." But Crick didn't change a thing. The model was correct.

While the contraption was large, it represented the structure of DNA, which is extremely small. Consider this. Your body is made up of some ten trillion cells. Chromosomes are inside each of the cells. DNA molecules are found in the chromosomes of all living cells and even in some viruses.

In a way, DNA molecules look like tiny springs coiled inside skinny threads—the chromosomes. If you could take out the DNA in one cell and stretch it, you'd find it was 6 feet (nearly 2 meters) long. If you could stretch out all of the DNA in all of your cells, you'd have a chain that was 50 trillion feet (15 trillion meters) long. That's longer than 20,000 trips to the moon and back!

Some 500 average-sized cells can fit inside the period at the end of this

James Watson (left) *and Francis Crick, seen with their model of part of a DNA molecule, showing its structure as a double helix.*

sentence. How do you see *inside* a chromosome that is *inside* a nucleus that is *inside* a cell? It's not easy.

By the 1950s, scientists were using electron microscopes, which could magnify a cell more than 200,000 times. Rosalind Franklin, who was also working at Cambridge University, took some of the first pictures of DNA. She used a process called X-ray diffraction crystallography. What she saw in the pictures were patterns of shadows.

Have you ever made shadow pictures against your bedroom wall—where you held your hands in front of a light in a certain way and you made images of rabbits? You knew they were rabbits. But if you had no idea what rabbits looked like or even what rabbits were, could you figure it out from the shadow pictures?

Somehow Franklin's blurry photographs helped Watson and Crick to crack the code of DNA. But they also had some other clues. In the 1940s, scientists had discovered that the DNA molecule consisted of phosphate and deoxyribose and four base compounds—adenine, cytosine, guanine, and thymine. Still, no one could figure out how these substances fit together. In 1952, chemist Linus Pauling and his associates figured out that DNA formed some sort of a spiral structure, something like a twisted rope. In 1953, using all this information, Watson and Crick came up with the correct structure—DNA was in the shape of a double helix. For their work, they won the Nobel Prize in 1962.

How did Watson and Crick figure out the DNA structure when it had stumped so many scientists before them? Great scientists use both knowledge and intuition. Einstein had said, "When I examine myself and my methods of thought, I come to the conclusion that the gift of fantasy has meant more to me than my talent for absorbing positive knowledge."

Let's give Watson the last word. He closes his book, *The Double Helix*, by quoting a painter: "The important thing is to be there when the picture is painted." Watson continues, "And this, it seems to me, is partly a matter of luck and partly good judgment, inspiration and persistent application."

The Central Dogma

After the structure of DNA was discovered, most biologists in the 1950s believed that all of the important genetic questions had been answered. DNA provided the genetic code, this code was translated to RNA, and this in turn became protein. It was simple and precise: DNA to RNA to protein. Scientists called it the central dogma.

In 1956, George Palade offered further proof of the central dogma. He found that RNA was located inside ribosomes, and this was where protein was manufactured.

Genes, said the molecular biologists, were like pearls on a string—they always remained in the same place. The scientists in this decade experimented with one of the simplest living organisms, a bacteria named *Escherichia coli*. One Nobel Prize winner reportedly said that what was true for *E. coli* would be true for the elephant. After all, these scientists explained, the central dogma was simple and precise.

They were wrong. The formation of the genetic code wasn't so simple. Not until 1961—when two men named François Jacob and Jacques-Lucien Monod said that something else was happening inside the cell—did the scientific community change the central dogma.

But one woman had known the central dogma was wrong all along. Three times during the 1950s, botanist Barbara McClintock had published her findings. The scientific community ignored her. One researcher described McClintock as an "old bag." Others claimed that she was "mad"—crazy.

What did Barbara McClintock know?

A Feeling for the Organism

Barbara McClintock knew that genes did not stay in place like pearls on a string. They jumped. The jumping genes moved from place to place on the thin threads of chromosomes. While the central dogma stated that the genetic code moved in one direction—from DNA to RNA to protein, McClintock said that the genetic code could move back and forth. While the central dogma claimed that all genetic code originated within the molecular structure of DNA, McClintock said that genetic instructions also came from the cell, the organism, and the environment. While molecular biologists claimed that most of the riddles of genetic inheritance had been solved, McClintock believed that the most interesting questions had not even been asked.

She was right. But how did she know? McClintock studied maize, or corn. She planted it. She watched it grow. She examined the shape of the leaves, the

Barbara McClintock in a photograph taken in 1983, the year she was awarded the Nobel Prize for physiology or medicine.

color of the kernels. "The important thing is to develop the capacity to see one kernel that is different, and make that understandable," she explained. "If [something] doesn't fit, there's a reason, and you find out what it is."

But perhaps most importantly, McClintock trusted her intuition, her "feeling for the organism." In one interview, McClintock explained that when she worked with the chromosomes, "I was right down there with them, and everything got big. . . . It surprised me because I actually felt as if I were right down there and these were my friends."

In 1983, McClintock won the Nobel Prize for the work that she had done in the 1950s. For years, because she was a woman, her work had been ignored. McClintock was not bitter. "When you feel that strongly about something," she said, "you can't be turned off. Nobody can hurt you. You just go right on. Nobody can hurt you."

SWEET DREAMS

Have you ever watched your dog taking a nap? Did you notice his feet moving, his nose twitching, and his eyes moving rapidly from side to side under his closed eyelids?

Believe it or not, your dog was in the middle of a dream. For all we know, your dog might have been dreaming about chasing rabbits.

In the fifties, psychologists studied people who were sleeping and made some interesting observations. For example, did you know that during deep sleep, your eyes move rapidly from side to side under your closed eyelids? Your breathing, heartbeat, and blood pressure rise to the same levels as if you were awake. Psychologists call this REM (rapid eye movement) sleep.

During REM sleep, you are most likely dreaming. If your REM sleep is interrupted over a period of nights, your body will suffer psychological stress. To stay healthy, it seems that your brain must dream at night.

Rachel Carson and *The Sea Around Us*

Quick, name a subject that most people like to read about. Did you think of the ocean?

In 1950, few people walked into a bookstore and asked for the ocean section. But this was before Rachel Carson published *The Sea Around Us*. In the summer of 1951, her book hit the *New York Times* best-seller list, and it stayed there for eighty-six weeks. That Christmas in a *New York Times* poll, readers voted it the "outstanding book of the year."

Carson showed people how their lives are affected by oceans, and how the oceans will become even more important as people begin to "destroy the land." Her prose read like poetry, and she wrote with heartfelt knowledge about the sea. "My mind has stored up everything I have ever learned about it as well as my own thoughts, impressions, and emotions," she explained.

Throughout the 1950s, people clamored for her books—in spite of the fact that Carson was a woman scientist. At the close of the decade, Carson began work on a book that was to change the course of history. In 1962, after the publication of *Silent Spring*, large pesticide companies set out to destroy Carson's credibility as a biologist.

Why? For the answer, you must turn to the decade of the 1960s.

4
CHEMISTRY

Chemistry is the scientific study of substances and their processes. In the 1950s, every scientific field benefited from the expertise of chemists. In this book, you'll see the contributions made by chemists to the fields of archaeology, biology, medicine, physics, and technology.

When you read the archaeology section, you discovered that a chemist developed radiocarbon dating. When you read the biology section, you found that biochemists figured out the molecular structure of DNA. When you read the physics section, you'll realize that a knowledge of chemistry helped produce the hydrogen bomb.

In the past, it seemed that scientists could solve their scientific puzzles by using the knowledge within their own fields. But in the 1950s, solving many of the scientific puzzles required knowledge in several fields.

Don't jump to the mistaken conclusion that scientists always agreed with one another. In the 1950s, science provoked fierce arguments. When you examine the arguments, you'll find that many of them had to do with chemistry.

If you've ever argued with your brother or sister, chances are good that in a couple of hours you worked out your differences. This didn't happen in the 1950s. The arguments dealt with such serious issues that even today, there are scientists who violently disagree with one another about them.

In this chapter, you'll read about these controversial issues: the effects of radiation, the use of pesticides, and the use of wonder drugs.

THE EFFECTS OF RADIATION

The major argument of the decade focused on the use of the nuclear bomb. Hundreds were exploded in tests both above and below ground. People began to get sick from radiation. Some died. Dairy cows ate contaminated grass, children drank milk from the cows, and the children suffered. Plants, animals, people—they all felt the effects of the radiation. Sometimes years passed before the illnesses showed up.

Nobel Prize winner and chemist Linus Pauling demanded that the tests be stopped. Don't detonate bombs, he pleaded. Because of his views, U.S. officials actually denied Pauling a passport to go to England for a scientific conference in 1952. (If he had been allowed to attend the conference, some claimed that Pauling might have been the one to solve the mystery of DNA.)

Edward Teller, the father of the hydrogen bomb, said that radioactive fallout (radioactive dust following an explosion) wasn't so serious. He claimed that it was the duty of scientists to pursue all knowledge to the fullest extent. He was still defending this idea in 1987 when he wrote, "I believed, and persisted in believing, in the possibility and the necessity of developing the thermonuclear bomb. My scientific duty demanded exploration of that possibility."

The U.S. government and the military, in their eagerness to be prepared for war, agreed with Teller. Declaring that "radiation is natural," the government continued exploding bombs, exposing soldiers and U.S. citizens to radiation. Over the next thirty years, some six thousand veterans filed health claims

Edward Teller is shown here relaxing with his family.

related to atom bomb tests; only one-fifth were approved. Finally, in 1988, Congress passed a bill granting health benefits to these "atomic veterans."

Troubled Waters

By the 1950s, chemists had come up with several chemical compounds that could kill insects. The U.S. government encouraged farmers to use pesticides on their crops. Even city officials used pesticides to poison mosquitoes and flies.

To be fair, their motives were sincere. The officials wanted to increase the production of food, and they wanted to prevent the spread of disease.

But environmentalists began to discover that the poisons also harmed plants, animals, and humans. The pesticides entered the water supply. Ask any fisherman who makes his living on a bay or a harbor, and he'll tell you the effects of poison on fish.

My husband grew up in Comanche County, Texas. During the 1950s, farmers throughout the county used pesticides on their peanut crops. Some forty years later, Comanche County has one of the highest rates of cancer among its citizens in the entire state.

By the end of the 1950s and after much debate, the U.S. government banned the use of DDT, a pesticide. The use of other pesticides, however, has continued.

KILLER FRIENDS

Are you a gardener? If you are, then you know that certain insects can really damage your plants. Before you reach for a chemical pesticide to kill those bugs, why don't you let some natural predators do your dirty work?

A praying mantis with its spiny front legs will eat any insect it can grab. A ladybug prefers to eat nasty aphids. A caterpillar-hunter wasp dines on caterpillars. A yellow jacket paralyzes a tobacco hornworm, cuts it into pieces, and then carries it back to its papery nest to feed its larvae.

A warty tree frog dines on crickets, while a jumping spider enjoys delicious treehoppers (insects that eat ornamental trees). A box turtle eats beetles. And baby birds prefer a snack of soft and juicy insects.

If you must use an insecticide, make sure you read the directions. Don't use products that have a skull and crossbones on the container. They can harm your health, and it's not worth the risk.

Even though laboratory studies have shown that pesticides cause cancer in rats, it's hard to prove that pesticides cause cancer in humans. It may take years before pesticide poison is detected in the human body. Also, since pesticide manufacturing companies earn millions of dollars, they can afford to hire the best lawyers for their defense.

It's tough to win a case against such companies. In 1966, when lawyer Victor Yannacone of Patchogue, Long Island, learned of massive numbers of dead fish turning up at Yaphank Lake, he and other environmentalists started filing lawsuits against polluters. Yannacone rarely won. Even so, he was satisfied when scientific evidence became part of the public record and when this knowledge educated people.

Perhaps the reason people have continued to use pesticides is ignorance. It is hard to believe that a pesticide that kills a bug might also hurt you.

WONDER DRUGS

In the 1950s, people called antibiotics wonder drugs. These chemical compounds killed off a variety of microorganisms, and without the use of them, many people died. One antibiotic, streptomycin, was used in the treatment of tuberculosis (TB). It was so successful that all over the country, TB hospitals began to close their doors. People recovered. In 1952, American Selman Waksman won the Nobel Prize for the discovery of streptomycin.

Unfortunately, there was a dark side to this story. By 1958, doctors were discovering that there was an increase in infections, particularly among hospital patients. Infections were becoming resistant to antibiotics. As a result, antibiotics did not always make someone healthy again.

By the 1990s, this problem was so severe that many medical officials fear that there will again be worldwide epidemics, and that they will have no medicines to protect people.

The testing of atomic bombs, the dangers of pesticides, and wonder drugs—these issues are only a small part of the study of chemistry. But, during the 1950s, these were the issues that people discussed and debated.

5

MEDICINE

Can you whistle the theme song of your favorite television show? A theme is a brief melody that recurs in a song; in a story, the theme is the main idea. By now, you've probably discovered that there are even themes for science in the 1950s. The decade was a time of hope, when some people believed that science could solve any problem. And the decade was a time of fear, when other people believed that science would destroy us all.

In the 1950s, the word *ethics* began to show up during discussions of science. The word *discovery* frequently pops up in science. In the 1950s, however, it seemed that people were beginning to question the morality of science, something that had rarely been considered before. A new theme began appearing—the theme of science and ethics.

This was certainly true in the field of medicine. We'll start with a review of some of the medical discoveries of the 1950s. Then, we'll take an in-depth look at one of the greatest achievements of the decade and of the twentieth century—best expressed in the words of newsman Edward R. Murrow: "Polio has been conquered!"

MEDICINE IN THE 1950S

Without a doubt, it was an extraordinary decade for medicine. In 1950, the drug reserpine was first used to treat high blood pressure. Because it calmed patients without putting them to sleep, reserpine was also used to treat schizophrenia, thereby making it one of the first tranquilizers available for the treatment of the mentally ill.

The medical procedure amniocentesis was developed in 1952 to test the health of an unborn baby still in the mother's womb. Also in that year, the world's first successful sex change operation was performed in Denmark.

After plastic surgery and doses of female hormones, American soldier George Jorgenson became "Christine."

In 1953, the heart-lung machine was used successfully for the first time, on an eighteen-year-old girl. Developed by American surgeon John Gibbons Jr., the invention took over the work of the heart and lungs during a heart operation.

At the beginning of the 1950s, artificial insemination was being used on cattle. Semen was extracted from a bull and then later inserted into a cow. This procedure impregnated cows. By 1953, artificial insemination was successfully used on three women, bringing new hope to couples with fertility problems.

That same year, researchers found that tars from tobacco smoke caused cancer in mice. In 1954, researchers reported that the death rate of heavy smokers was twice that of nonsmokers. (Still, it took years before the general population accepted that smoking was harmful.)

In 1955, medical scientists announced that severe alcoholism shrinks the brain. In 1956, the first dialysis machine was used on a patient with malfunctioning kidneys. It wasn't a pleasant experience; several times a day and for long hours, the patient was hooked up to a machine that flushed the kidneys, but it beat the alternative. As a result of the invention of the dialysis machine, thousands of lives were saved.

Alick Isaacs and Jean Lindemann discovered interferon in 1957. At the beginning of an infection, this protein molecule is produced in the body and protects it from any additional viruses. By the 1990s, medical scientists were manufacturing interferon and using it to treat some forms of cancer.

Also in the 1950s, thousands of people bought their first pair of contact lenses. Now, people whose vision needed correction could choose between contacts and glasses.

Another medical achievement of the 1950s was the birth control pill. It was developed in 1951, tested in Puerto Rico in 1956, and by 1959, the "pill" was on the market. In a way, the pill helped usher in the cultural revolution of the 1960s as people began to change their way of living.

Many people in the 1950s believed that medical scientists would cure the common cold by the end of the decade, but unfortunately, the cold is still around. The researchers certainly tried. (Soldiers were usually the guinea pigs.) In 1950, scientists developed antihistamines, which relieved the symp-

THE FIGHT AGAINST TOOTH DECAY

In 1950, a penicillin tooth powder went on the market. It was expected to prevent tooth decay, but it was eventually removed from store shelves because it didn't work.

Fluoridation was more successful. After discovering that people had fewer cavities if their drinking water had fluoride, cities began to fluoridate water supplies. This resulted in fewer cavities for the general population.

toms of colds and allergies. In 1957, they came up with a vaccine for the flu. And, in 1958, scientists announced that the common cold could be prevented if patients took weekly injections prepared from the bacteria of their own noses and throats. People of the 1950s were more than willing to stick contacts in their eyes, but they balked at collecting stuff from their noses and getting shot with it.

There was one shot, however, that people did not mind getting at all. It was the polio vaccine.

Polio Pioneers

In the spring and early summer of 1954, some two million schoolchildren stood in line and waited their turns for a shot. First-, second-, and third-grade students wore their best clothes and had their hair neatly combed. They felt excited and proud. There were a few who were afraid, of course, but they bit their lips and quickly wiped their eyes. After all, each one of them had a job to do. The adults couldn't do it; they needed the help of the children—the Polio Pioneers.

Poliomyelitis (from the Greek words that mean "gray marrow") is a virus that attacks the brain and spinal cord. It causes paralysis. At one time, doctors mistakenly believed that only children could get it, and the disease was called infantile paralysis. But polio can strike anyone.

Polio is not a new disease, but it struck the twentieth century hard. The virus lives in human excrement, and since ancient people were not particularly sanitary, they built up an immunity to the virus. Modern people with improved sanitary practices did not have this immunity and were vulnerable to the disease.

Polio terrified people. They thought the virus came into the body

Young Polio Pioneers proudly did their part in the poliomyelitis vaccine field trials.

through the nose and mouth (it did), but they weren't sure. Everywhere parents warned their children—don't play with anyone. Don't go swimming in the town pool. Don't drink from the water fountain.

People with mild cases of polio suffered from stiff necks and backs and then recovered. Those with severe cases lost the use of their arms and legs forever. Others lost the use of their lungs and had to lie inside a huge device called an iron lung, which helped them to breathe. The people with the worst cases died.

Beginning in 1916, not one year passed without a major polio epidemic somewhere in the world. In 1952, polio attacked nearly 50,000 Americans. It was time to do something about it.

The Search for a Cure

Jonas Salk was already at work. Polio affects the nerve cells, but researchers before Salk had discovered that in the early stages of the disease, the virus circulates via the bloodstream. This was good news because it meant that a shot would be an effective method of vaccination.

One of Salk's first tasks was to get monkeys. Before 1949, the only way of producing the virus was infecting monkeys and then killing them. By 1949, however, scientists had learned how to produce the virus in the laboratory without using animals.

Another problem was to figure out how many different strains of polio there were. Scientists discovered one hundred. In 1951, Salk and his staff realized that the one hundred strains fell into three categories: Type I, Type II, and Type III. They also realized that if a vaccine was produced with the main types, it would provide protection from all the strains.

A cautious man, Salk developed a "killed-virus" vaccine. He did not want to inoculate people with a live vaccine, for fear that something would go wrong. So, he killed the poliovirus in a formaldehyde solution. Tests showed that it was dead after three days; Salk kept it in the solution for thirteen days.

Salk conducted his first tests on himself and his family. He gave a series of four shots—one for each main type of polio and a booster. Then, in the summer of 1952, Dr. Salk tested his vaccine on some patients at the D. T. Watson Home for Crippled Children at Leetsdale, Pennsylvania. No one got sick. Instead, the children developed stronger antibodies, strong enough to fight off further exposures to polio.

When Salk announced the results of his tests, people cheered. A Gallup Poll showed that more Americans knew about the poliomyelitis vaccine field trials than knew the name of the president. (It was Dwight D. Eisenhower.)

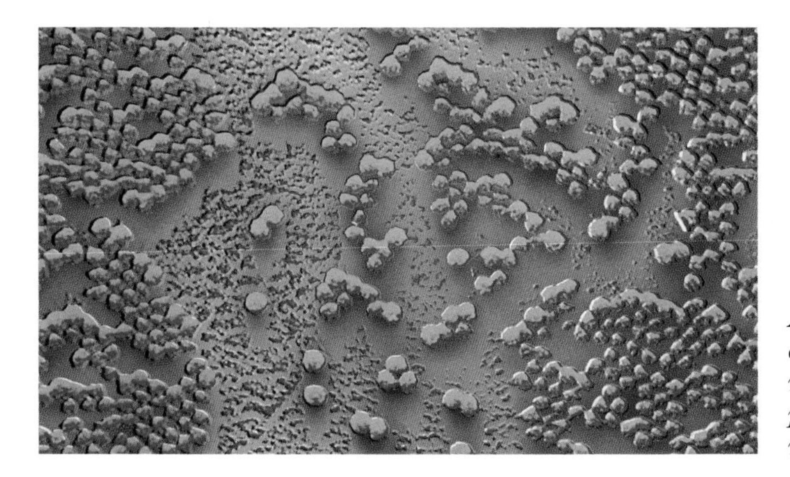

A color-enhanced micrograph—a photograph taken through a microscope — of polio virus particles which have been magnified thousands of times

In the spring of 1954, when some two million children brought home notes from school inviting them to "participate" in an experiment, parents eagerly signed. All across the country, young students learned the procedures of a scientific experiment.

Every child would receive three shots at three different times. Half of the children received the real vaccine. Half received placebos, shots that looked (and felt) exactly like the real vaccine but weren't. Records would be kept for one year to determine if any of them caught polio. The following year, the children who received the placebo shots would then receive the real vaccine.

After each shot, the Polio Pioneers received lollipops. After their third shot, they also received large buttons and wallet-sized cards announcing I WAS A POLIO PIONEER.

This mammoth experiment was not without some crises. Companies all over the country were producing the polio vaccine, and some of them were not as careful as Dr. Salk. Because of mistakes made by Cutter Laboratories in California, some children caught polio after they were vaccinated.

As a whole, Jonas Salk's vaccination program was an outstanding success. The United States government paid for the vaccines. Medical personnel donated their time to administer the vaccine. School officials offered the use of their buildings. PTA mothers trooped around in the rain to collect the written permission slips. With such a spirit of cooperation—with people helping people—the program succeeded.

On April 12, 1955, the Salk vaccine was officially licensed for use in the United States. The polio scare was over.

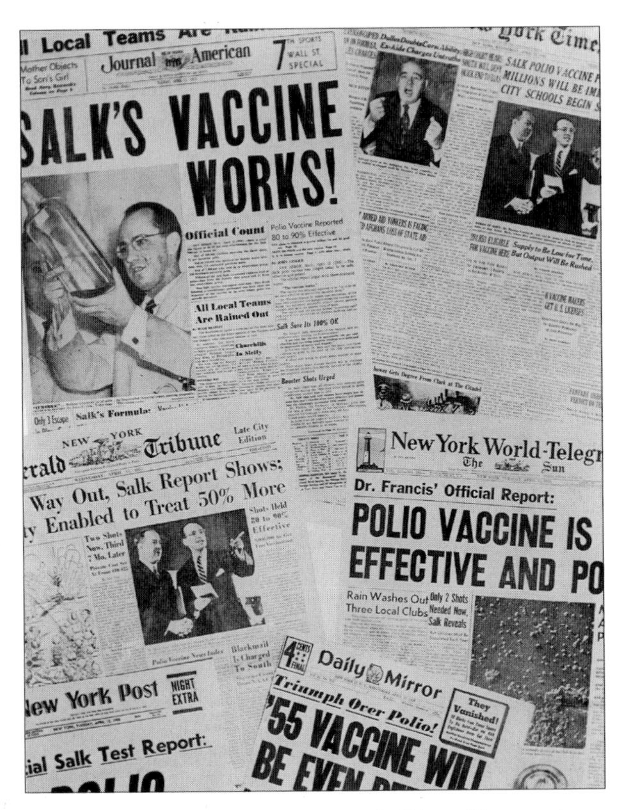

America rejoiced when Jonas Salk's polio vaccine was proven to be a success.

VOICES OF AMERICA, 1953

"When I was growing up in Wisconsin, in Oshkosh, my mother would never let me go to the State Fair. I always wanted to go, but she'd say, 'Do you want to get polio and spend your life in an iron lung?' What a terrifying thing that was—the iron lung."

"Parents in Los Angeles were terrified of polio. There had been some very bad epidemics there. I remember riding my bicycle around and around the block, because I wasn't allowed to play with anybody."

"Polio? That was the big fear when I was young—especially growing up in the South. You didn't want to be anywhere near it. In 1952, we still didn't have TV in Shreveport [Louisiana]. I remember going to Dallas [Texas] and seeing television for the first time. In the news every day was a tally of the polio cases—like today they total up the car crashes on holiday weekends. Every day they would report 'another so many polio cases today.' That was my first sense of what news was."

"Just today, I was bending over to take a drink from a fountain. The water wouldn't go up, there was just a trickle over the spout, and I heard my mother's voice saying, 'Don't drink that—you'll get polio.' It was just a flash from my childhood."

from: *Patenting the Sun: Polio, the Salk Vaccine, and the Children of the Baby Boom* by Jane S. Smith (New York: Morrow, 1990).

Jonas Salk refused to patent the polio vaccine. He refused to take money for it. When newsman Edward R. Murrow asked why, Salk replied that the patent belonged to the people. "Could you patent the sun?" he asked.

When another interviewer asked how it felt to have achieved such success, Salk replied, "To a scientist, fame is neither an end nor even a means to an end. Do you recall what Emerson said?—'The reward of a thing well done is the opportunity to do more.' "

Albert Sabin's Oral Vaccine

Albert Sabin scoffed at Dr. Salk's "killed-virus" theory. Sabin declared that only a weakened "live-virus" vaccine would be effective against polio over many years. Sabin rarely missed an opportunity to humiliate Salk. But being rude does not mean you can't be a great scientist.

Sabin produced a weakened "live-virus" vaccine, using polio strains that were too weak to cause paralysis. He had discovered that the vaccine could be ingested, meaning that a person could swallow it and get protection from polio. But in the late 1950s, still enchanted with Jonas Salk, people didn't pay much attention to Sabin.

Albert Sabin tested his oral polio vaccine in Russia. It was approved for use in the United States two years later.

So, in 1959, Sabin worked with the Russians and tested his vaccine on some four million people. It worked.

It also worked in attracting the attention of the U.S. government. The Sabin polio vaccine was easier to administer than the Salk vaccine; people took it orally, swallowing the vaccine instead of getting shots. And, the Sabin vaccine lasted longer than the Salk vaccine.

In 1961, the United States provided the Sabin vaccine to its citizens. At three different times, my family went to the elementary school I attended. We were handed a little white paper cup with a sugar cube. The vaccine was on the sugar. It tasted like sugar. No one in my family ever caught polio.

Today, polio is no longer a worldwide epidemic. Doctors give babies and young children a series of doses of the oral Sabin vaccine. As a result, they are immune to polio for the rest of their lives.

The fifties were a time of hope, when some people believed that science could solve any problem. Jonas Salk, Albert Sabin, and thousands of doctors and nurses made one hope a reality for us all.

6

PHYSICS

Children, theologians, and physicists often ask the very same questions. What keeps the clouds up? Is there an order to the universe? How did the world begin?

Physics touches every field—astronomy, biology, chemistry, and mathematics. In many respects, it is the grandest of all the sciences. Physics is the art of understanding why.

Art requires curiosity, knowledge, and flashes of intuition. But in 1950, physicists appeared a little short on insight.

Just five years earlier, they had accomplished the impossible; they had split the atom. Yet in 1950, physicists still had no idea what the atom looked like. What's more, the theories that they had accepted and had based their experiments on for the past thirty years weren't working.

And whether or not they admitted it, the physicists who worked on the atomic bomb had to confront the consequences of their actions. Had physics gone astray? After all, physicists had used their "art" and had created an instrument for mass murder.

In the 1950s, physics reached a turning point. It needed new flashes of intuition, new insights. In this chapter, we'll look at some of the people who provided those insights. We'll look at their discoveries. And we'll look at their moral dilemmas.

THAT TINY ATOM

Pluck a hair from your head. Now, stretch it out and look at it. An atom is more than a million times smaller than the thickness of that single strand of hair.

What's more, an atom is composed of even smaller particles. Protons and neutrons are found in the nucleus of the atom. The nucleus is more than 100,000 times smaller than the atom itself.

In 1945, U.S. nuclear physicists managed to manipulate what went on inside the tiny nuclei of atoms. They created the atomic bomb.

Suddenly, people realized that nuclear physics had powerful consequences. In 1951, Sir John Douglas Cockcroft and Ernest Thomas Sinton Walton won the Nobel Prize in physics for building a machine called a particle accelerator, which could produce nuclear disintegrations.

Keep in mind the size of an atom. With the particle accelerator, Cockcroft and Walton succeeded in bombarding an atom with protons. Faster than you can blink your eyes, the structure of the atom's nucleus changed, or disintegrated, by emitting particles.

Nobody had paid much attention to Cockcroft and Walton's work during the 1930s and 1940s. But finally, when the prize was awarded in 1951, people snapped to attention. Newspaper headlines used a catchier phrase for the particle accelerator. They called it an atom smasher.

How do you smash an atom that is a million times smaller than the thickness of a hair? Secondly, how can you see what you've done? The physicists of the 1950s, eager to answer these questions, came up with some amazing solutions.

The Field Ion Microscope

Erwin W. Muller wanted to see an atom for himself. For years, this German-born American physicist experimented with different types of microscopes. At last, he created the most powerful magnifying instrument in the world—the field ion microscope. In 1951, Muller took the world's first picture of atoms.

While Muller called his invention a microscope, it certainly didn't look like one. Some scientists called Muller's invention a field ion emission imaging machine. With such a name, you know that the "picture" didn't look like the ones you get developed at the drugstore.

To get an image of atoms, Muller enclosed a needle and a fluorescent screen in an airless glass tube with a small amount of helium gas. He then applied up to 30,000 volts of electricity to the needle.

The needle was 1,000 times sharper than the tip of an ordinary pin. When the needle was pointed toward the fluorescent screen, the screen showed an enlarged image of the tip of the needle. The image looked like a bunch of small circles. These circles were actually the arrangement of atoms on the tip of the needle.

Picture a lace doily that sits under a table lamp and you have a pretty good idea of Muller's first image of atoms. At best, the image was too fuzzy to see individual atoms. Still, the field ion microscope was a remarkable achievement.

The Bubble Chamber

While Erwin W. Muller was looking at the outside of the atom, Donald Glaser was concentrating on the inside.

Remember that an atom is more than a million times smaller than the thickness of one hair, and that the nucleus is more than 100,000 times smaller than the atom. At present, it is still impossible to actually see inside the nucleus of the atom.

In 1953, Donald Glaser did the next best thing. He invented the bubble chamber and photographed the tracks of particles *inside* the atom—protons, neutrons, and electrons—called subatomic particles.

Since the 1920s, physicists had been using C. T. R. Wilson's cloud chamber to figure out what went on inside the atom. Think of a cloud chamber as a sort of container of humid air with a moveable piston on top. The humid air forms a tiny cloud where charged subatomic particles speed along and have collisions. The particles create paths of small droplets of liquid. The paths are then photographed and studied. In this way, scientists learned about the inside of the atom.

Donald Glaser used a different method in his bubble chamber. He heated a liquid to the boiling point. In the bubble chamber, the speeding charged particles of the boiling liquid didn't produce droplets along their paths; they produced bubbles.

The first bubble chamber was only a few inches big, but it had two advantages. One, it gave a sharper picture than a cloud chamber. Two, a greater number of collisions occurred in the bubble chamber and that gave physicists more details to study in the pictures.

As soon as Donald Glaser shared his bubble chamber design with other scientists, they began to use it. They also began to improve it.

In 1954, Luis Alvarez used liquid hydrogen instead of boiling liquid in his bubble chamber. This gave an even clearer image of the "bubble path." He then developed a bigger bubble chamber. By the end of the decade, Alvarez had a 72-inch (183-centimeter) bubble chamber up and running.

READING A BUBBLE PATH PHOTOGRAPH

In bubble path photographs, each particle has its own unique "signature." The electrons make faint wiggly lines. Protons leave thick straight lines. Positively charged particles bend one way. Negatively charged particles bend the other. Neutral particles don't leave a path at all.

By studying these photographs, physicists determined the life span of the particles. These life spans were so short that the particles moved, left their bubble paths, and decayed in less time than it takes to blink your eyes.

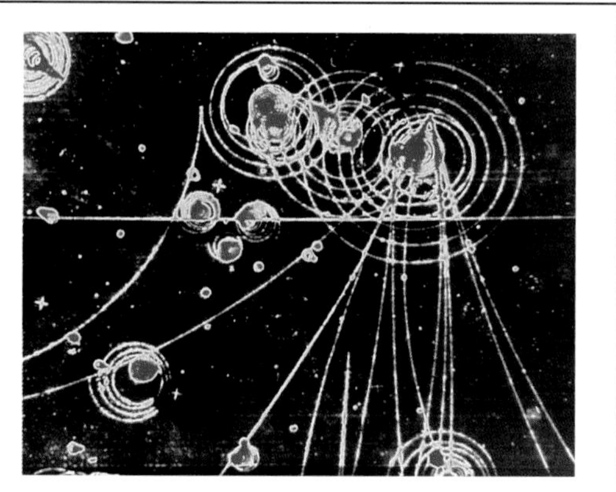

Particle tracks produced when a high speed proton strikes an atom

THE FRANCKENSTEIN

Just one experiment with a bubble chamber could produce 50,000 photographs. In the early 1950s, physicists working at Brookhaven National Laboratory on Long Island, New York, hired housewives to analyze the pictures. The women worked around the clock in three shifts seven days a week. They enlarged the film, spread it out on white tabletops, and then sketched the thousands of swirly lines. After that, they measured the angles and lengths of all the lines in their sketches.

The work was boring and slow. Scientists needed a quicker way to analyze bubble chamber findings. In 1955, Luis Alvarez came up with a solution. Why not use a computer?

Scanners at work inspecting film from bubble chamber photographs

he asked. In 1956, using Alvarez's ideas, Hugh Bradner and Jack Franck built a computer called the Franckenstein.

This semiautomatic measuring machine analyzed bubble chamber findings—fast. Eventually, the Franckenstein was replaced by improved machines, but the basic principle of how they worked remained the same.

The Bevatron

Keep in mind that in order to "see" subatomic particles, you have to smash atoms. In other words, the atoms have to collide and break apart.

Physicists began working on new and improved particle accelerators. In 1954, scientists at the University of California at Berkeley developed a particle accelerator called the Bevatron. The Bevatron accelerated protons to an energy of five to six billion electron volts (BeV).

What particles did the physicists see? They saw protons. They saw electrons. And they saw particles that completely baffled them.

Antiparticles

In the 1930s, physicist Paul Dirac had worked out a mathematical theory that suggested that for every subatomic particle there must also be its exact opposite. Scientists had already discovered the antielectron, or positron. In 1955, Emilio Segrè and Owen Chamberlain discovered a negatively charged particle with the mass of a proton. They called it an antiproton.

Finding an antiproton was no easy task. For hours, Segrè and Chamberlain bombarded copper with particles and produced some 250 antiprotons. For each antiproton they identified, some 40,000 other particles came into existance.

A year later, in 1956, physicists detected antineutrons. They also discovered neutrinos, massless particles with interesting properties. (Right now, at this very moment, neutrinos are zipping through your body.)

How do antiparticles affect your daily life? Most physicists would be quick to answer that they don't affect your life one way or another. But it is theoretically possible that there could be an antiworld. This world would be exactly opposite to ours. In this antiworld, there would be a person who was your opposite.

Of course, most physicists scoff at this idea. Still, the theory makes an intriguing science fiction plot for a book or a movie.

Strangeness

Since the physicists had suspected that antiprotons existed, they were not particularly surprised when they found them. But there were other subatomic particles that puzzled the physicists. These unknown particles left a new kind of bubble path. They also decayed more slowly than other particles the scientists had seen.

Because physicist Murray Gell-Mann disliked complicated scientific language, he simply said that these new particles were strange particles. This name stuck. Although Murray Gell-Mann studied the strange particles for the rest of the decade, he didn't have much luck in figuring out what they were.

By the 1960s, however, Gell-Mann would have the answer. He proved that some of the basic theories of physics had been wrong. The neutron, proton, and electron were not the smallest particles in the atom. Instead, these particles were made up of even tinier particles. And in keeping with his love of language, Gell-Mann named his tiny new hypothetical particles quarks.

But we are getting ahead of our story. While *quark* is a funny-sounding word, there was a different word that came to people's minds in the 1950s when they thought of physics. It was not a funny word.

The word was *H-bomb*.

The Father of the Hydrogen Bomb

He was a short man with big bushy eyebrows. He loved sweets. He liked to play the piano. During the 1950s, his photograph appeared in magazines and newspapers. In some photographs, the man with the bushy eyebrows smiled and played with children. People called him the father of the H-bomb. His name was Edward Teller.

The hydrogen bomb is the most destructive weapon in the world. It is highly explosive, and its radioactive fallout has the potential to kill millions of people.

Unlike the atomic bomb, which is based on fission (the splitting apart) of atoms, the hydrogen bomb requires fusion (the joining together) of atoms.

First, uranium atoms are split apart, releasing energy and creating a temperature of millions of degrees. This fission process violently sets off the fusion of heavy forms of hydrogen, which in turn produces helium. The mass lost in this combining process is turned into energy as explained by Einstein's famous equation $E = mc^2$. (This is a simple explanation of a very complex operation.)

On November 1, 1952, the United States detonated the world's first hydrogen bomb on Elugelab, a mile-wide island on the Eniwetok Atoll. Elugelab was part of the Marshall Islands, a territory of thirty-four small islands in the central Pacific Ocean governed by the United States. Code-named Mike, the bomb was a 65-ton (58-metric-ton) monster. It looked like a giant thermos bottle—two stories high and 6 feet (nearly 2 meters) wide.

The H-bomb exploded with a force of 10.4 megatons. It was 700 times more powerful than the bomb that was dropped on Hiroshima.

The island of Elugelab disappeared forever.

On August 12, 1953, the Russians exploded their version of the hydrogen bomb.

The United States government detonated the first of six planned tests on Bikini Atoll, also part of the Marshall Islands, on March 1, 1954. Code-named Bravo, the first bomb was a 15-ton (14-metric-ton) explosive that destroyed all life for nearly 200 square miles (520 square kilometers).

Unexpectedly, the wind shifted during the test and put three inhabited islands and 250 people in the path of the fallout. The ocean fish became radioactive. One hundred miles (160 kilometers) away, gray white ash rained down on a small Japanese fishing boat, the *Lucky Dragon*. The twenty-three crew members became sick with nausea, diarrhea, and vomiting; they did not know what was happening to them. Six months later, crew member Aikichi Kuboyama died. He was the world's first hydrogen bomb victim.

Despite mounting evidence, Teller claimed that radioactivity was not a serious danger. Nobel Prize-winning chemist Linus Pauling disagreed. Robert Oppenheimer, the physicist in charge of building the atomic bomb, had already stated his views on the subject. Two months after the explosion of the A-bomb, Oppenheimer resigned his position, declaring, "the physicists have known sin." The scientific community was sharply divided.

The general public was afraid. Would there be an atomic war?

When I was a girl in the fifties, we practiced duck-and-cover drills at school. The alarm sounded; we jumped from our desks, huddled on the floor, and covered the back of our necks with our hands.

I used to worry about what would happen if the bomb dropped. Could I find my little sister in her classroom? How fast could we run home? Would I be able to find my mother and father? How long would the radioactivity last?

In the 1950s, it was Teller's belief and the United States government's policy that the country should stockpile nuclear weapons. In 1955, the United States had some 4,000 atomic bombs and the Soviet Union had 1,000, enough to kill everyone on earth several times over. Supposedly, the fear of being bombed would prevent another war. This policy remained in effect for almost thirty years, until finally both the Americans and the Russians agreed to begin dismantling their weapons.

But a large quantity of uranium that the United States stockpiled for bombs has disappeared. Who has it, and what do they intend to do with it?

Was Edward Teller right, or was he wrong?

YOU DECIDE—GOOD MAN OR EVIL?

Two Nobel Prize-winning physicists had this to say about their colleague Edward Teller. Eugene P. Wigner said, "He is the most imaginative person I have ever met, and this means a great deal when you consider that I knew Einstein."

On the other hand, I. I. Rabi said, "[Teller] is a danger to all that is important. . . . I do really feel it would have been a better world without Teller. . . . I think he is an enemy of humanity."

THE *NAUTILUS*

They called it the *Nautilus*. Smooth and sleek, it was 300 feet (90 meters) long, weighed 2,800 tons (2,540 metric tons), and cost $55 million. It could travel 30,000 miles (48,000 kilometers) without refueling, and it could cross an ocean in five or six days without ever coming to the surface. In 1954, with Admiral Hyman G. Rickover at the helm, the United States Navy launched the *Nautilus*, the world's first atomic-powered submarine.

Ordinarily, the U.S. Navy named new submarines for those that had sunk during World War II. But the world's first atomic submarine was no ordinary ship. It was named after the submarine in Jules Verne's classic story *Twenty Thousand Leagues Under the Sea*.

On its first trip, the *Nautilus* broke all records for speed and for time underwater. In 1958, it sailed under the ice of the North Pole. Few people believed that it was possible to build an atomic-powered submarine, and it probably would have remained impossible except for the hardworking and demanding Admiral Rickover.

After World War II, Rickover longed for a peacetime navy. He longed to use atomic energy for good, not bad. And that's just exactly what the stubborn Admiral Rickover did when he navigated the oceans in the world's first atomic submarine.

The Law of Conservation of Parity

Have you ever argued with your parents? Did you prove to them that they were wrong and that you were right? Did you get a prize for winning the argument?

In a manner of speaking, that's exactly what two young physicists did. They proved that the thirty-year-old theory of the law of conservation of parity was wrong. As a result, in 1957, they won the Nobel Prize.

The phrase—the law of conservation of parity—is a mouthful. What's more, it's tricky to explain and tricky to understand.

In physics, *parity* is a mathematical term that implies even or odd. In the 1950s, physicists said that a particle could have even parity or it could have odd parity, but it couldn't have both at the same time.

The law of conservation of parity is based on the principle that inside atoms you can't tell right from left. In other words, right and left are always symmetrical; the mirror image is exactly the same as the real event.

But the physicists of the 1950s had a problem. Two of the recently discovered strange atomic particles, tau and theta, weren't behaving according to this law. They were exactly alike, except one had even parity and one had odd parity. Physicists called it the theta-tau puzzle.

Two Chinese-American physicists, Tsung-Dao "T. D." Lee and Chen Ning "Frank" Yang proved that the law was wrong. They said that inside atoms there *was* a difference between right and left. Theta and tau were two different particles.

In May 1956, over a cup of tea at a Chinese restaurant in New York City, Yang and Lee had an argument. For them, arguing was a way to think out loud and to learn from each other. A month (and several more arguments) later,

Lee and Yang came up with their theory. Since they were both theoretical physicists and not laboratory physicists, American physicist Chien Shiung Wu conducted the experiments that would prove if Yang and Lee were right. By December 1956, she had proof. Lee and Yang's theory was correct.

Yang and Lee were asked if they celebrated when they learned that their idea had been proven correct. Yang replied, "No. Joy was not paramount in our minds. At that time, we felt an intense excitement, because so many questions could now be asked, so many answers were ready to be approached."

Richard Feynman—The Intuitive Genius of the 1950s

Richard Feynman never learned his left hand from his right; he had to look at a mole on one of his hands to tell the difference. He played the bongo drums. He learned how to pick locks. He taught himself to locate people by smell, like a dog sniffing at a trail. Feynman was an interesting fellow, and without a doubt, he was one of the greatest intuitive physicists of modern times.

When other physicists were getting bogged down in mathematical problems and theories, Feynman leaped to the heart of the matter. Feynman explained. He told stories. He drew diagrams (later called Feynman diagrams) that covered the chalkboard. His diagrams looked like the wire mesh of chicken coops, yet somehow they illustrated the confusing ideas of waves and particles in a way that words could not. Dr. Feynman had a hand in most of the solutions to the physics problems of the 1950s.

When Feynman finally won the Nobel Prize in 1965, he was interviewed by a reporter. The reporter asked him to explain, in one minute or less, why he had won the Nobel Prize. Feynman replied, "Listen, buddy, if I could tell you in a minute what I did, it wouldn't be worth the Nobel Prize."

7

TECHNOLOGY

Technology is the practical application of knowledge. While that's a simple definition, most people have no idea how things work. Ask a friend to define technology, and he or she just might say, "It's magic."

In the 1950s, there were all sorts of technological inventions that certainly seemed magical. In this decade, millions of Americans bought their first televisions sets. They ate their first frozen TV dinners. Home freezers went on sale.

For Christmas 1954, the Regency Company sold some 100,000 new gadgets called transistor radios—forever changing retail shopping at Christmastime. In 1955, Velcro was patented, although it was nearly thirty years before the noisy stuff showed up on tennis shoes.

At theaters, people watched 3-D (three-dimensional) movies. To get the full effect, they wore special glasses.

These were just a few of the technological inventions of the 1950s. It's hard to study technology by itself. After all, technology is the application of knowledge from one or more scientific fields. You've already read about jet planes, satellites, and submarines.

In this chapter, we'll concentrate on these areas: computers, transistors, integrated circuits, xerography, and television. But just for fun, we'll start off with a look at how people in the 1950s imagined life in the year 2000.

LIFE IN THE YEAR 2000

It's always fun to think about the future. It's especially fun to read what someone from the past wrote about *us*. In January 1952, *Popular Mechanics* ran a story describing life in the year 2000. The story featured the Dobsons, an imaginary family in a town called Tottenville. Consider yourself the expert on life in the twenty-first century. Which things did the writer Waldemar Kaempffert get right, and which things did he miss?

The airport is at the center of Tottenville, with the streets extending from the airport like spokes on a wheel. Roads in the year 2000 aren't narrow, and they don't have any curves. Instead, they are wide and straight. Highways are double-decked, with the upper decks reserved for fast nonstop traffic.

Electric "suns" on huge towers light up the town at night. But an atomic power plant doesn't generate the town's energy. Even in the 1950s, scientists knew that atomic plants weren't economical.

The Dobsons' house cost just $5,000. Wood and bricks are out of the question; they are too expensive. Instead, walls are metal and floors are poured plastic. The roof is flat and holds several inches of water, which helps keep the house cool.

To cook, Mrs. Dobson uses an invention called the electronic industrial stove, which thaws a steak in eight seconds. There's no dishwasher. Disposable dishes melt under hot water.

To clean house, Mrs. Dobson turns on the hose and sprays their plastic furniture. The water runs down a drain in the center of the floor. Mrs. Dobson doesn't have to wash many clothes. The family's rayon underwear is bought by chemical factories and turned into candy.

Of course, television is an important part of daily living. Mr. Dobson uses it for business conferences. Mrs. Dobson uses it to shop.

Well, expert, what do you have to say about life in the year 2000 as imagined by a writer in 1952?

COMPUTERS

Certain touchstone words and phrases describe the fifties. One touchstone word was *fear*. Because of experiments with the hydrogen bomb, because of the cold war, and because of the threat of polio, people knew fear.

Yet strangely enough, another touchstone word for the fifties was *anticipation*. People anticipated that technology was on the brink of making the impossible possible. The future, people believed, held technological wonders.

The wonders, however, were still in the future, and this was particularly true with computers. In the 1940s, computers were the size of football fields.

They were big, noisy, hot, and expensive, and needless to say, nobody had a computer sitting on their desk at home.

This was still true in the 1950s. Each computer was custom ordered and cost nearly a half million dollars. In 1953, IBM was so proud of the small size of its 701 computer that it bragged that each section of the 701 could fit inside an elevator and go through a door.

The fifties, at least for computers, linked the past to the future. The impossible became closer to becoming possible because of scientists such as Alan Turing, J. Presper Eckert Jr., John W. Mauchly, and Grace Hopper.

Artificial Intelligence

In 1951, Allan Turing (who helped crack the German secret code during World War II) wrote an article called "Can a Machine Think?"

The answer was yes. Scientists coined the term *artificial intelligence.* If you could carry on a conversation with a computer and in some way the computer responded, then artificial intelligence had been displayed.

Scientists began to look for ways to demonstrate artificial intelligence. In 1954, the first patent for a robot was issued. In 1956, the first computer chess program, Maniac I, beat its human opponent in a game.

Eckert and Mauchly

As we've already mentioned, 1940 computers were big. They needed miles of wire and thousands of tubes. They were, however, extremely fast. The ENIAC (Electronic Numerical Integrator and Computer) could add 5,000 ten-digit numbers in one second.

But there was a catch to this speed. The computer had no memory. Every time the computer had to solve a different kind of problem, it had to be rewired. What's more, a new program had to be written, and this could take months.

The answer, of course, was to build a machine that had a memory for both data and programs. And that's exactly what J. Presper Eckert Jr. and John W. Mauchly did. They called it the Universal Automatic Computer, or UNIVAC.

Building UNIVAC was no easy feat. Eckert and Mauchly started work in

J. Presper Eckert Jr., at the controls of the UNIVAC

1946 and didn't deliver their first computer until 1951. Both men lived on the brink of financial disaster. They endured ridicule. Computer expert Howard Aiken claimed that "there will never be enough problems, enough work for more than one or two of these computers," and that Eckert and Mauchly should "stop this foolishness."

The two men ignored the advice. To get money, they sold their company to Remington Rand, which later became Sperry Rand. In 1953, the Rand UNIVAC was the only computer on the market. But IBM took over the market with an aggressive sales and service policy. The Rand corporation, unwilling to sink more money into computers, fell behind. So did other computer companies. People called the takeover "IBM and the Seven Dwarfs."

Trouble just wouldn't seem to go away. Eckert and Mauchly spent most of their remaining years either fighting in court over their computer patents or in delaying those court battles. Some twenty years later, lawyers for John Atanasoff—the man who in 1939 had built the first semielectronic digital computer—accused Eckert and Mauchly of stealing Atanasoff's ideas.

All of this trouble was the result of one thing. The UNIVAC was a commercial success.

What was so special about the UNIVAC computer? In 1951, when the first UNIVAC rolled into the U.S. Bureau of the Census, the units still looked big and bulky. But lo and behold, the UNIVAC did not have to be rewired for each problem. It processed numerical data. It processed alphabetical data. It printed bills, solved problems, and it even predicted elections.

In 1952, television network executives decided to use the UNIVAC to predict the outcome of the presidential election. Newsman Walter Cronkite said, "Actually, we're not depending too much on this machine. It may be just a sideshow . . . and then it may turn out to be of great value to some people."

When the computer programmers announced that the UNIVAC predicted Eisenhower would win, the television executives panicked. As fast as possible, the programmers reprogrammed the UNIVAC, entering false data so that the UNIVAC would predict a narrow race between Eisenhower and his opponent, Adlai Stevenson. Those were the results that were announced over the air.

But the UNIVAC was right. Eisenhower won the race. "The trouble with machines," said Edward R. Murrow, "is people."

Grace Hopper

Amazing Grace, as her friends called her, would have said amen to Murrow's statement. Grace Hopper is considered one of the great computer pioneers. During World War II, Hopper, who had been a mathematics professor, joined the United States Navy. She wanted to help her country, and that's just exactly what she did—for the next forty years.

During the war, Hopper was a programmer for the Mark I, one of the early gigantic computers. After the war, she worked on ways to make the computer easier to program. By 1951, she had come up with a device called a compiler. The compiler translated English commands into a code that the computer could understand.

Imagine giving instructions to a computer in ordinary English instead of punching in long numerical codes! Impossible, people said. A computer can't understand English. Some computer programmers worried about what would happen to their jobs if just anybody could work a computer.

Lieutenant Grace Hopper works at a manual tape punch machine early in her long career.

Hopper grew tired of hearing the phrase "but we've always done it that way" from people who questioned her ideas. She claimed that the phrase was "the worst in the English language."

But her friends didn't call her Amazing Grace for nothing. The compiler worked. During the rest of the fifties, other scientists worked on improving it. In 1957, IBM introduced FORTRAN, a computer language in English. (The term stood for "formula translation.") In 1959, Hopper developed COBOL, which is still used by computer programmers today.

In 1992, Grace Hopper died at the age of eighty-five. She once said that she hoped to live until the year 2000. "I have two reasons," she explained. "The first is that the party on December 31, 1999, will be a New Year's Eve party to end all New Year's Eve parties. The second is that I want to point back to the early days of computers and say to all the doubters, 'See? We told you the computer could do all that.' "

Transistors

In 1956, Walter Brattain, John Bardeen, and William Shockley received the Nobel Prize for inventing the transistor. When they had created it nine years earlier at the Bell Laboratories in New Jersey, no one paid much attention. In fact, the *New York Herald Tribune* claimed that the "spectacular aspects of the device are more technical than popular."

For a while at least, that statement was true. Early in the decade, the U.S. military insisted on computers with tubes instead of transistors. They had "always done it that way," and they did, after all, know what to do when the tubes burned out. The U.S. Army, using the ENIAC computer to compute artillery trajectories during World War II, actually ordered soldiers to stand around the ENIAC while they held baskets of tubes and watched the computer. When a tube burned out, the soldiers rushed in to replace it.

But the transistor was an incredible invention, and within the decade, it began to replace the tube, and this in turn led to even more inventions.

So, what exactly is a transistor, and why was it so important? First, let's look at its importance.

As we've already said, computers in the 1950s were fast. They could have gone even faster, but what slowed them down were those miles of wires and tubes. They had some 18,000 tubes and several thousand connection points. Just think of all the things that could go wrong—besides the tubes burning out.

The transistor (formed from two words—*trans*, which means "across," and *resist*, which means "to fend off or to withstand") served the same function as the tube. Very simply, the transistor conducted the electrical current. It was small, cheap, and fast. Even the early transistors switched on and off twenty times faster than tubes.

The transistor was based on a completely new idea in physics. For a long time, scientists had used copper and iron because they were good conductors of electricity. But Shockley and his team used a semiconductor material, a material that did not conduct electricity so well. After some experimenting, they settled on silicon. Silicon, a nonmetallic chemical element, is one of the most common elements in the world. Sand is made up of silicon.

Shockley and his team wanted to control electrical current. By experimenting, they discovered that in order to control the current, the atoms of silicon they worked with should be in the form of crystals. They also discovered that some impurities needed to be added to these crystals. The impurities controlled the way the electricity flowed. Some types of impurities added extra electrons (n-type). Other types of impurities didn't add electrons, and this resulted in holes in the material (p-type).

The first transistor looked like a blob of clay with some wires sticking out of it. But once Shockley and his team figured out the basic idea, they found a more sophisticated way of making transistors. They used silicon crystals and sliced them. (Remember that these are very tiny slices.) They exposed some of the slices to the n-type impurities and some to the p-type impurities.

Think of a sandwich—two pieces of skinny bread and an even skinnier piece of cheese. To make an NPN sandwich, you use two slices of n-type "bread," the stuff that has extra electrons, and you use a slice of p-type "cheese," the stuff that has holes. One of the outside slices is the emitter. The other outside slice is the collector. The inside slice is the base. Attach some wires to this tiny sandwich, stick it in a tiny case, and you've got yourself a junction transistor.

The junction transistor not only turned the electrical current off and on, but it also controlled the amount of current and where it went. The transistor did not need as much power as a tube needed. It amplified the signal (made it stronger) in the electrical current. It did not give off much heat, and it was quiet.

By 1952, a hearing aid with a junction transistor was on the market. In 1954, transistor radios were the hit of the Christmas season. If scientists could make a radio so small that it would fit in your pocket, people thought, then maybe it was actually possible to make a computer that would fit on a desk.

Newspapers called these "midget radios" in 1953. Developed by Radio Corporation of America, the smaller radio weighed only a pound. Six miniature flashlight batteries would keep the larger radio playing for about 500 hours.

Integrated Circuits

Summer in Texas is hot, and it's a good time to get out of the office and go on vacation. In July of 1958, that's exactly what everyone did at Texas Instruments in Dallas. That is, everyone except for Jack Kilby.

Kilby, an electronic engineer, had been at the company for just two months. He didn't have any vacation time. So, for two weeks, he had the lab to himself. And he was determined to make good use of his days.

A methodical, patient man, Kilby didn't mind working on a problem and coming up with a hundred different solutions, as long as he found one solution that worked. "A lot of solutions fail," he explained, "because they're solving the wrong problem, and nobody realizes that until the patent is filed and they've built the thing."

He also believed in watching costs. "You could design a nuclear-powered baby bottle warmer," he said, "and it might work, but it's not an engineering solution. It won't make sense in terms of cost."

In the hot Texas summer, Kilby started thinking about integrated circuits. He thought about how to make them simpler and cheaper.

A circuit is an unbroken path for electrical current. The transistor sends signals through these electric circuits. In 1958, every time you wanted the computer to perform a different function, you needed another transistor and another electric circuit. Why, asked Kilby, couldn't you build an integrated circuit that could perform the work of many circuits? So, he did it.

Five months later, in California, Bob Noyce basically came up with the same idea. While their companies fought for years over who owned the integrated circuit, Kilby and Noyce good-naturedly shared the credit with each other.

By the 1960s, other scientists started figuring out ways in which to use integrated circuits. Just to give you a brief preview of some of their inventions—think pocket calculators, electronic watches, and rockets.

Xerography

Today, you can find a copier just about anywhere—schools, libraries, stores, and offices. I even have one at home. But in the fifties, this wasn't the case. In those days, teachers didn't pass out photocopied worksheets; students had to copy their assignments from the chalkboard. If you wanted to copy something from a library book, you had to write it out by hand.

Frankly, if it hadn't been for Chester F. Carlson, we might still be copying things by hand. Carlson worked in a New York patent office, and whenever he needed copies of long reports, he either had to find someone to type up a copy or he had to pay for an expensive photostat.

Carlson decided there was only one thing to do. He marched to the New York Public Library and started reading everything he could find on photoconductivity (which has to do with transmitting electricity and exposure to light) and electrostatics (a branch of physics that deals with objects charged with electricity).

In 1937, Carlson applied for a patent, and by 1938, he had created the world's first dry, electrostatic copier. Carlson called his machine an electrophotographic apparatus. Nobody was interested.

By the 1940s, a small company had agreed to take on the project. One of the company officials thought that electrophotographic apparatus was a mouthful, so he asked a language professor to come up with an alternate name. The professor put two Greek words together that meant "dry writing" and came up with a brand-new word—*xerography*.

In 1955, the Haloid Company bought out Carlson and the first company. Haloid was determined to manufacture a copy machine using Carlson's idea. Short of money, Haloid workers had plenty of imagination. Their first test models consisted of old tire pumps, drainpipes, and rabbit hair.

By 1959, the company had a new name—the Haloid-Xerox Company—and it had a genuine Xerox machine on the market. The company called it the 914. (It could handle sheets of paper up to 9 by 14 inches (23 by 36 centimeters). The size of a large desk, the 914 weighed 648 pounds (294 kilograms) and cost $29,500.

Haloid-Xerox officials were so eager for business, they told customers that they didn't have to buy the 914; they could lease it for just $95 a month. What's more, the first 2,000 copies were free, the additional copies would

TYPING TRIVIA

- In 1956, at her kitchen table in Dallas, Texas, Bette Nesmith mixed up some white paint and put it into tiny bottles. For years, she had painted over her typing errors, and she figured that other typists might want to do the same. When IBM told her that it wasn't interested in her idea, Nesmith and her young son went into business in their kitchen. Their product, Liquid Paper, made them millionaires. (Michael Nesmith grew up to star in "The Monkees" television show and to become one of the first producers of music videos.)
- A voice-operated typewriter was also developed in 1956. The newfangled machine didn't catch on with the public.

cost just a nickel each, and to top it all off, when the 914 broke down, Haloid-Xerox would come and repair it.

The Xerox machine was on its way.

TELEVISION

Here's the nutshell definition of your television. The television camera records the action. The picture is divided into several hundred thousand tiny parts in a process called scanning. This information is translated into light and sound waves, and these are transferred into electronic signals.

The electronic signals are then transmitted and broadcast to your house. Your television receives the signals and decodes everything. An electron gun inside your television scans the screen, and when the gun hits tiny phosphor dots on the screen, the dots glow and form the color picture.

The first person to demonstrate the possibilities of television was Vladimir Kosma Zworykin. In the winter of 1923-1924, Zworykin (a Russian who moved to America) showed off his invention to Westinghouse. One of the first programs was a cartoon of Felix the Cat. Felix, unfortunately, was a little fuzzy.

A radio company, Radio Corporation of America (RCA), decided to get into the television business. In 1936, RCA placed television sets in 150 homes in New York City and began broadcasting. When World War II came along, however, television was put on hold.

Soon after the war, the television business started picking up speed. In 1947, some nineteen stations went on the air. In 1948, the first television studio was built, in Baltimore, Maryland. And for the first time, in 1951, there was a coast-to-coast telecast. People all over the United States watched President Truman give a speech at the Japanese Peace Treaty Conference in San Francisco.

MR. POTATO HEAD

The first children's toy was advertised on television in 1952. It was Mr. Potato Head. At first, kids stuck an assortment of noses, ears, eyes, and hats into a real potato. But soon, for safety's sake, a plastic potato with holes was included with the package. Over the next forty years, some fifty million Mr. Potato Heads were sold.

In those years, everything was live. Technicians began figuring out ways to tape shows so that they could be broadcast at another time. They actually invented the videocassette recorder. Still, it took nearly thirty years before the VCR was available for the home market.

In 1951, some shows were telecast in color. But the price of a color television was not within most families' budgets. People put off buying color televisions until the sixties.

While black-and-white televisions weren't cheap, most people in the early fifties managed to buy sets. Television fascinated them. They watched Milton Berle in "The Texaco Star Theater" and Lucille Ball in "I Love Lucy." Children sang along with the "Howdy Doody" theme song.

In 1950, six million Americans owned TV sets. By 1960, sixty million Americans owned televisions.

No doubt about it—television is great entertainment. You can laugh. You can cry. You can learn things. Most people, however, have a tendency to watch too much.

Computers, transistors, copy machines, and televisions—the fifties was an important decade for technology. When I was a girl, these were amazing, magical machines. Just imagine the technological wonders of the next millennium. What stories will you tell your grandchildren about the good old days of the twentieth century?

Television took America by storm in the 1950s. Six million *Americans owned sets at the start of the decade; by the decade's end, that number would be increased ten-fold, to* sixty million.

Further Reading

Bredeson, Carmen. *Jonas Salk: Discoverer of the Polio Vaccine.* Hillside, N.J.: Enslow, 1993.

Cole, Michael D. *John Glenn: Astronaut and Senator.* Hillside, N.J.: Enslow, 1993.

Harlan, Judith. *Rachel Carson: Sounding the Alarm.* New York: Macmillan, 1989.

Heiligman, Deborah. *Mary Leakey: In Search of Human Beginings.* New York: Scientific American Books for Young Readers, 1995.

Liptak, Karen. *Dating Dinosaurs and Other Old Things.* Brookfield, Conn.: Millbrook, 1992.

Reef, Catherine. *Rachel Carson: The Wonder of Nature.* New York: Twenty-First Century Books, 1992.

———. *Jacques Cousteau: Champion of the Sea.* New York; Twenty-First Century Books, 1992.

Ronen, Avraham. *Stones and Bones! How Archaeologists Trace Human Origins.* Minneapolis: Lerner, 1993.

Whitelaw, Nancy. *Grace Hopper: Programming Pioneer.* New York: Scientific American Books for Young Readers, 1995.

Wilcox, Frank H. *DNA: The Thread of Life.* Minneapolis: Lerner, 1988.

Willis, Delta. *The Leakey Family: Leaders in the Search for Human Origins.* New York: Facts on File, 1992.

Yount, Lisa. *Pesticides.* San Diego: Lucent, 1994.

Index

References to illustrations are listed in ***italic, boldface*** type.

airplanes, 24–25, 30, 63
Alvarez, Luis, 56, 57
amniocentesis, 45
antibiotics, 33, 44
antihistamines, 46
antiparticles, 57, 58
artificial insemination, 46
astronauts, ***30***, 31
atomic bomb, 10, 43, 44, 53, 54, 58, 59, 60. *See also* hydrogen bomb; nuclear bomb.
atoms, 53, 54, 55, ***56***, 58, 61

big bang theory, 17, 23, 24
birth control pill, 46
Brattain, Walter, 68
bubble chamber, 55, 56, ***56***

cancer, 43, 44, 46
carbon-14, 9, 10
Carlson, Chester F., 71, 72
Carson, Rachel, 34, 39
chromosomes, 35, 36, 37, 38
COBOL, 68
computers, 63, 64–65, 66–67, 68, 71, 74
  ENIAC, 69
  Mark I, 67
  UNIVAC, 65, ***66***, 66–67
Cousteau, Jacques, 33
Crab Nebula, ***19***, 20
Crick, Francis, 35, ***35***, 36

deoxyribonucleic acid (DNA), 33, 34–35, ***35***, 36, 41, 42
Dirac, Paul, 57

Eckert, J. Presper, Jr., 65, 66, ***66***
Eisenhower, President Dwight D., 28, 29, 31, 49, 67
electrons, 55, 56, 57, 58, 69
Escherichia coli (E. coli), 37
Explorer 1, 29–31

FORTRAN, 68
Franklin, Rosalind, 36

Gell-Mann, Murray, 58
genetic code, 34, 37
Glenn, John H., Jr., 26, ***30***, 31

Hopper, Grace, 65, 67, ***68***, 68
Hoyle, Fred, 23, 24
Hubble, Edwin, 22, 23
Hubble Space Telescope, 18
humans, 9, 24, 25, 34, 42, 43, 44
  ancient, 10, 12, 13, 15, 16
  space travel of, 26, 31
hydrogen, 18, 56, 59
hydrogen bomb, 41, 42, 58, 59, 64. *See also* atomic bomb.

IBM, 65, 66, 68, 72
integrated circuits, 63, 71
International Geophysical Year (IGY), 28

Kilby, Jack, 70, 71

Laika, 28, ***28***
Leakey, Louis and Mary, ***15***, 15
Lee, Tsung-Deo, 61, 62
Libby, Willard, 9, 10, 11, ***11***
Lovell, Bernard, 20, 21, ***21***, 22, 24, 28

mathematics, 53, 57, 61, 67
Mauchly, John W., 65, 66
McClintock, Barbara, 34, 37, 38, ***38***
Mediterranean Sea, 9, 12, 13
microscopes, 54
  electron, 36
  field ion, 54, 55
Milky Way galaxy, 18–19, ***19***
Muller, Erwin W., 54, 55
Murrow, Edward R., 45, 51, 67

National Aeronautics and Space Administration (NASA), 31
Nautilus, 60, 61
Nesmith, Bette, 72
neutrons, 54, 55, 58
nuclear bomb, 41. *See also* atomic bomb.
Nutcracker Man, 16. *See also Zinjanthropus boisei.*

Oppenheimer, Robert, 59
Orion Nebula, 20

parthenogenesis, 33
particle accelerator, 54
Pauling, Linus, 36, 42, 59
pesticides, 39, 41, 43, 44
Pickering, William, ***29***
pilots, test, 24, 25, 26, 31
polio, 45, 47, 48, 49, ***49***, 50, 51, 52, 64
Polio Pioneers, 47, ***48***, 50
polio vaccine, 47, 49, 50, ***50***, 51, 52
protons, 53, 54, 55, 56, ***56***, 57, 58

quarks, 58

radiation, 18, 20, 21, 31, 41, 42
Radio Corporation of America (RCA), 73
radioactive fallout, 42, 58
radioactivity, 10, 59, 60
radiocarbon. *See* carbon-14.
radiocarbon dating, 9, 10, 11, 12, 14, 41

Reber, Grote, 20
reserpine, 45
ribonucleic acid (RNA), 37
ribosomes, 37
Rickover, Admiral Hyman G., 60, 61
rockets, 26, 29, 30, 31, 71
Rogers, Alan E. L., 20
Rutherford, Ernest, 10

Sabin, Albert, 51, 52, ***52***
Salk, Jonas, 48, 49, 50, 51, 52
Sandage, Allan, 22, 24
satellites, artificial, 29, 63. *See also Sputnik 1* and *Sputnik 2*.
Sea Around Us, The, 39
Segrè, Emilio, 57
sex change operations, 45–46
Shepard, Alan B., Jr., 31
Shockley, William, 68, 69, 70
Silent Spring, 39
space age, 17, 27, 28
Sputnik 1, 17, 26, 27, ***27***, 28, 30, 31
Sputnik 2, 28, ***28***
stars, 17, 20, 21, 22
steady state theory, 17, 23–24
strange particles, 58
subatomic particles, 55

telescopes, 18, 20
  optical, 18, 20, 21, 22
  radio, 18, 20, 21, 22, 28
television, 63, 64, 73–74, ***74***
Teller, Edward, 42, ***42***, 58, 59, 60
transistor radios, 63, 70, ***70***
transistors, 63, 68, 69, 70, 71, 74
Turing, Alan, 65

Van Allen, James, ***29***, 31
Van Allen radiation belts, 31
Ventris, Michael, 12, 13
von Braun, Wernher, 29, ***29***

Watson, James D., 35, ***35***, 36
World War II, 20, 69, 73

xerography, 63, 71–73

Yang, Chen Ning, 61, 62
Yeager, Chuck, 25

Zinjanthropus boisei ***15***, 15. *See also* Nutcracker Man.
Zworykin, Vladimir Kosma, 73

About the Author

Mona Kerby and her husband, both Texans, live in New Windsor, Maryland. For years, Ms. Kerby was the librarian at J. B. Elementary School in Arlington, Texas. She is now the Coordinator of the Graduate School Library Media Program at Western Maryland College in Westminster, Maryland.

Ms. Kerby is the author of *Thirty-eight Weeks Till Summer Vacation*, which won Minnesota's Maud Hart Lovelace Award for Young Readers in 1994. She has also written science books and biographies for young readers. This is her first book for Twenty-First Century Books.